D1444341

Managing the Web-Based Enterprise

Withdrawn

Managing the Web-Based Enterprise

Jesse Feiler

Morgan Kaufmann

AN IMPRINT OF ACADEMIC PRESS
A Harcourt Science and Technology Company

San Diego San Francisco New York Boston
London Sydney Tokyo

This book is printed on acid-free paper.

ACADEMIC PRESS
A Harcourt Science and Technology Company
525 B Street, Suite 1900, San Diego, CA 92101-4495 USA
http://www.academicpress.com

Academic Press
Harcourt Place, 32 Jamestown Road, London, NW1 7BY, UK

Morgan Kaufmann Publishers
340 Pine Street, Sixth Floor, San Francisco, CA 94104-3205 USA
http://www.mkp.com

Library of Congress Card Number: 00-106358
International Standard Book Number: 0-12-251339-8

Printed in the United States of America
00 01 02 03 04 IP 9 8 7 6 5 4 3 2 1

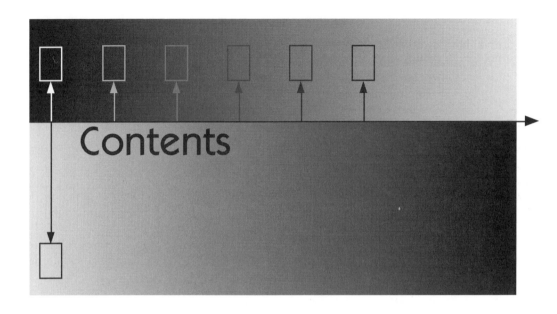

Contents

Foreword	xix
Preface	xxi
Who Should Read This Book	xxii
How This Book Is Organized	xxii
Part I: The Web-Based Enterprise	xxii
Part II: Sites and Pages: Design and Maintenance	xxii
Part III: Staffing and Managing the Web-Based Enterprise	xxiii
Related Books	xxiii
For More Information…	xxiii
Acknowledgments	xxiii

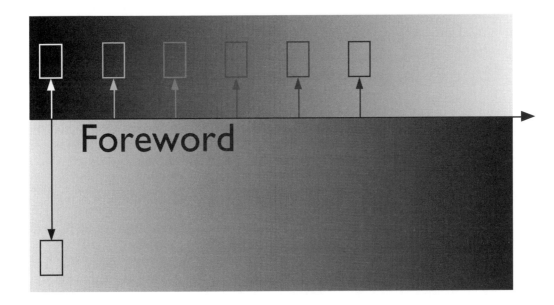

Foreword

Developing and managing large business systems for organizations such as the Federal Reserve Bank of New York and Merrill Lynch wasn't easy, but one part of the process was never called into question. When you have a project that may extend over a period of several years, with a budget that represents a considerable amount of an organization's technology expenditures, and that employs a significant number of the company's programmers, no one questions the need for aggressive, thorough, and effective management.

The ease with which Web pages can be developed and the apparent ease with which an organization can go "on the Web" sometimes belie the fact that these efforts, too, require aggressive, thorough, and effective management. Managing these projects and the Web-based enterprise in general doesn't require scaling down the corporate mainframe techniques; it requires new techniques that address the particular issues that arise in a Web-based enterprise. Those issues include the obvious ones of rapid development and the ease with which results—good, bad, or indifferent—can be achieved.

In the end, though, good management is good management. It focuses on objectives, results, the people who do the work—and the people who use the product. This book helps you achieve those results in the world of the Web-based enterprise.

BARBARA BUTLER

Barbara Butler has been an information technology professional for more than 20 years. The systems she has designed and managed have covered such aspects of the financial services industry as securities and funds processing, global banking activities, operations, financial processes, research and analytical efforts, administration, and human resources. She studied IT management at Harvard and earned her master's degree in organizational psychology from Columbia.

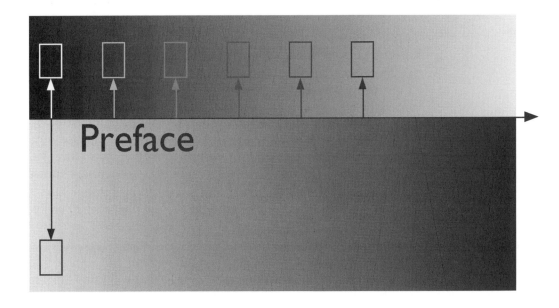

Preface

This book is a what-to-do, hands-on guide to creating and managing a Web-based enterprise. The book contains samples and templates—both of Web pages, HTML, and management documents such as job descriptions. They can be used to put together the basics of a Web-based enterprise by filling in the blanks and modifying highlighted areas. The annotations show what matters—and what doesn't; what can be copied blindly, and what requires thought, discussion, and decision-making. The detailed step-by-step project plan in the appendix lets you plan both the initial site development and its maintenance without letting pieces fall through the cracks.

Who Should Read This Book

This book is for people who are responsible for Web-based enterprises. The book provides a managerial roadmap to site design and maintenance. It nevertheless contains significant samples and templates of actual HTML, Perl, and JavaScript code that can be used as the basis for a site. Webmasters will learn what the issues confronting their managers are and how to deal with them while managers will learn what matters—and doesn't—in Web site design, maintenance, and evaluation.

How This Book Is Organized

There are three parts to the book.

Part I: The Web-Based Enterprise	This part of the book is an overview of the Web-based enterprise and the issues that affect it. A Web-based enterprise is not just an organization with a Web site (or even several Web sites); it is a new type of organization in which the Web and the aspects of the Web are integrated into all of its endeavors.
Part II: Sites and Pages: Design and Maintenance	The second part of the book shows you how to talk about, design, develop, and maintain the sites and pages of the Web-based enterprise. It presents a functional description of sites and pages that lets your categorize and speak about them in terms that are understandable to managers, programmers, users, and designers.

| Part III: Staffing and Managing the Web-Based Enterprise | As with any organization, the human capital is the largest investment for most Web-based enterprises. This part of the book deals with issues affecting the staff: recruiting and training as well as job descriptions and evaluations. It concludes with an overview of the steps to take in order to create and maintain a successful Web-based enterprise. |

Related Books

Database-Driven Web Sites and *Application Servers: Powering the Web-Based Enterprise* provide information on other aspects of the Web-based enterprise. The first focuses on data and the second on operations.

For More Information...

You can find more information on this topic together with updates to this book on the author's Web site. It is located at www.philmontmill.com.

Acknowledgments

At Morgan Kaufmann, Julie Bolduc, senior production editor, has worked her usual magic in making the production process move quickly and painlessly to completion. Mary Prescott, copy editor, and Gary Ragaglia, cover designer, have once again contributed immeasurably to the book.

Ken Morton guided this book through its development; Thomas Park and Carole McClendon added helpful comments and suggestions. Anthony Meadow of Bear River Associates provided insightful suggestions on the project. Sheri Dean instigated this book with a chance comment in a meeting at Morgan Kaufmann.

This book was written and produced on Macintosh computers using Adobe FrameMaker, Mac OS 9, and Mac OS X. Other products used include Adobe Photoshop, FileMaker Pro, Flash-It, FreeHand, Microsoft Word, Microsoft Windows, VirtualPC, and AppleWorks.

Notwithstanding the assistance from so many people, any errors remain the author's.

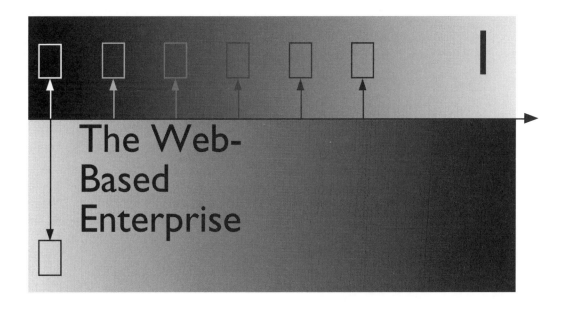

The Web-Based Enterprise

This part of the book provides an overview of Web-based enterprises along with basics of how and where people use the Web along with what they do on the Web when they get there. It lays out the range of possibilities for a Web-based enterprise and—most important—defines just what a Web-based enterprise is.

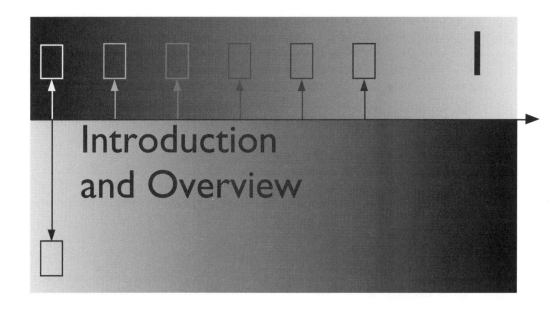

Introduction and Overview

This chapter describes the Web-based enterprise and how it works. The rest of the book shows you how to get here from wherever you may be, but in its descriptions, this chapter differs from the prescriptions of the rest of the book. Do not be discouraged if you recognize your organization only vaguely in this description: by the end of the book you will realize what parts of this are relevant to your organization and how to make your goals a reality.

Even if you are familiar with the Internet and the Web, you should read this chapter to familiarize yourself with the terminology used throughout this book. Many of the terms are quite standard; however, others—including Web size, Web time, and Web-based enterprise—are not widely used and in some cases are unique to this book.

The chapter consists of three sections:

- *"What Is a Web-Based Enterprise?" provides a definition of the new entity known as a Web-based enterprise.*

- *"The Growth and Development of Web-Based Enterprises" describes the ways in which Web-based enterprises can grow and develop: as start-ups, as enhancements to traditional enterprises, and as skunk-works projects that need to be taken control of.*

- *"Oranizational Origins of Web-Based Enterprises" explores the organization structures from which a Web presence typically evolves. Success of a Web-based enterprise is dependent on integrating the organization's entire structure into the Web-based enterprise.*

What Is a Web-Based Enterprise?

The Web burst on the scene in the late 1990s. It was first proposed as a research project at CERN in March of 1989[1], but for most people it entered their consciousness with the access provided through consumer-oriented Internet systems such as America Online, Prodigy, and CompuServe (starting in 1996). The financial world jumped on the "dot-com" bandwagon with a vengeance thereafter, and Jeffrey Bezos, founder of amazon.com, found himself on the cover of *Time* as Man of the Year in 1999.

The Web changes everything it touches, from the people who surf its varied pages to the people who post those pages. The Web-based enterprise is an enterprise that has been touched by the Web. The feeling is much like that of a wader in the sea who is knocked down by an unexpected wave: sputtering, the drenched soul stands up, brushing off sand and saying,

---

1. http://www.w3.org/History/1989/proposal.html

"What was that?" "That" is the Web for the drenched and disoriented organization. An organization that uses the Web quickly finds that it is a Web-based enterprise: the Web is at the core of what it does and how it does it. The use of the Web quickly pervades an organization and affects activities far removed from the Web itself.

Of course, not every organization goes through this process. Some cling tenaciously—desperately—to their pre-Web ways of doing things. But, just as with waders at the beach who try to remain standing in the face of the waves, organizations that ride the waves can master them.

A Web-based enterprise is an integrated operation in which the Web and traditional media are part of a unified and consistent organization. An organization that uses the Web quickly finds that it is a Web-based enterprise: the Web is at the core of what it does and how it does it. The use of the Web quickly pervades an organization and affects its activities far removed from the Web itself.

Remember that this does not always happen or does not happen efficiently and productively: that is why you are reading this book.

In this way, the Web becomes central to an organization that starts to use it. You have probably experienced this for yourself: within a relatively brief period of time after you started to use e-mail, you probably began to reduce your phone calls and paper-based communications. The power and efficiency of the Internet quickly overwhelm less powerful and efficient technologies.

Strictly speaking, the technologies described in this book go beyond the Web; they cover all of the Internet technologies. The Web, however, is what has made the Internet accessible to people far and wide. The ability to combine descriptive information on a Web page with other Internet technologies makes those technologies (such as e-mail and file transfer) easier to use from Web pages.

In addition to the one obvious characteristic—the use of the Web—Web-based enterprises share several attributes among themselves: they function in an environment with certain characteristics, and they continually move back and forth between the virtual and bricks-and-mortar worlds.

Attributes of Web-Based Enterprises

Beyond the use of the Web, Web-based enterprises share these four attributes:

1. They are Web-size organizations.

2. They function in Web time.

3. The are located in Web space.

4. They are flexible.

Not all Web-based enterprises fully appreciate the significance of these attributes, and not all implement them successfully. This section describes the attributes, and the rest of the book helps you implement them successfully in your organization.

Web-Size Organizations

A Web-size organization is the size of the Web. Any of the hundreds of millions of Web users can access the organization's information and can form a relationship of some sort with the organization. Web size is elusive, though. The Web itself provides this phenomenal connectivity; its pages, however, are each of modest size. You cannot tell from a single page or even from an entire site whether you are visiting General Motors or a local garage. Thus, Web size means a size that cannot be determined from the external cues of traditional entities in the real world. The actual size is less important than the fact that it is difficult to know just what the size is.

Why This Matters   A host of cues tell people about the builders of buildings, wearers of clothes, and purveyors of all sorts of goods. The marble columns in a traditional bank, the lofty (wasted?) space in a grand cathedral or department store, or the fuzzy bodice in the illustration on the cover of a dime novel—all of these provide cues to the discerning person.

On the Web, however, everything is virtual: no bodices are fuzzy and no space is any loftier than any other. All Web marble is faux. This means that traditional cues to the size and nature of an organization do not apply. Furthermore, since the Web is global, culturally specific cues are irrelevant and even harmful. All that matters is content and service.

This is a very difficult concept for some people and organizations to grasp. The solidity and reputation of traditional organizations have little value in many cases on the way.

To be sure, some of the attributes of traditional organizations are quite important on the Web. Particularly when it comes to financial dealings, you may be more inclined to patronize a financial organization of which you have heard. In other cases, however, people tend to decide whether or not to engage in business or other relations with an organization based on the content and presentation of that content on the Web site. The role of decoration for its own sake is quite limited.

Web Time

Web time is the now-proverbial 24/7—24 hours a day, 7 days a week. Middle of the night repairs to your Web site are likely to be midafternoon (and thus highly visible) repairs to a Web surfer on the other side of the world.

Not only is Web time 24/7, it also is fast. People increasingly expect to find and use information on the Web within minutes rather than days (or weeks). This can cause problems within an organization that is not used to functioning at this speed.

In extreme cases, an organization's Web team will respond an order of magnitude faster than its traditional response team.

Why This Matters Once you start to move your organization toward the Web, you are accepting Web time with its constant availability and its lightning-fast speed. Web time quickly pervades the organization; if it does not, resentment quickly arises between the Web team (who may consider themselves overworked) and traditional teams (who may consider the Web team hyperactive and even crazy). Worse, customers and clients may start to differentiate between the Web side of an organization and the traditional side; this type of scenario quickly divides the organization in two. A successful Web-based enterprise integrates the Web into all of its operations so that such a schism is not created.

Web Space

No one has a snapshot of a friend standing in front of the Web. You can see parts of the Web such as its routers, cables, and computers, but there is no center to the Web and no place to take such a snapshot. The Web is virtual, existing only in the ephemeral electrons of its transmissions.

Why This Matters The importance of Web space cannot be overestimated. From the helpless governments that are unable to tax transactions from virtual offshore corporations to the telecommuting webmasters who maintain Web sites worldwide from cabins in deep woods or cubicles in offices located in indistinguishable business districts, location no longer matters in the degree to which it once did.

The real estate agent's mantra of the three determinants of value ("Location, location, location") is apropos. The world is experiencing a rapid change in which space, location, and proximity are becoming more important for personal reasons than for business or professional ones. In this sense, Silicon Valley is an example of the pre-Web world.

Flexibility

Finally, Web-based enterprises are flexible. Flexibility extends to all aspects of their operations including personnel and management structures, operations, and client/user/public relations.

For example, many traditional organizations have formal or informal guidelines with regard to communications among employees. A typical guideline is that an employee can communicate directly to a supervisor or supervisor's supervisor. This prevents the CEO from being bombarded with memos appealing edicts with regard to African violets on windowsills and other issues of that ilk. However, in an environment in which people do not think twice about sending e-mail messages to the president of France (http://www.elysee.fr/mel/mel_.htm) or of the United States (president@whitehouse.gov), it is a little strange to suggest—much less implement—policies born of an age in which the writing, reading, and sending of correspondence were much bigger tasks than they are today.

Why This Matters People expect flexibility from Web-based enterprises. The moment that your organization dips its foot in the Web with its first tentative home page, people expect it to be updated, and they rapidly expect it to be complete. The Web (more accurately its hundreds of millions of users) abhors mysteries.

Flexibility extends from the design and implementation of Web sites to the organizations that support them. To some people, the notion of putting up a Web site is akin to putting up a marble-columned building: it is built for eternity. On the contrary, Web sites are built for the moment. Well-designed sites employ tools such as databases and application servers to allow the constant changes to be made without disruption. Likewise, Web-based enterprises know that they must design for certain types of changes and not be blindsided by circumstances that cause them to make changes that need not be made.

The World of Web-Based Enterprises

The world in which Web-based enterprises operate is characterized by five important points:

1. Globalization

2. E-commerce

3. Disintermediation

4. Life in the digital world

5. Support for bricks-and-mortar life

Globalization

The forces of globalization are intricately tied to the world of Web-based enterprises. The Internet, with its disregard for national boundaries, is an integral part of the globalized world.

E-Commerce

Each year, economists predict an enormous increase in e-commerce over the previous year. And each year, the economists' estimates prove to be too low.

Disintermediation

This word (originally coined by economists) refers to the ability of the Internet to bypass all sorts of intermediaries such as secretaries, librarians, receptionists, and others. You can send e-mail to the pope or the president of the United States; they may not read your messages, but you know how to find them. In practical terms, disintermediation means not so much eliminating all intermediaries; rather, it means eliminating many of them. You are likely to come closer to the person or information that you want on your own than you would in the traditional (intermediated) world.

Take as an example any organization that receives a large amount of input. In the traditional organization, the letters are opened and sorted by clerks. Each letter is scanned at least once to determine how it should be routed.

Some letters are discarded at this point. The remaining letters are passed on to people who can deal with them either directly or indirectly. These steps may be repeated at several places within the organization: scanning/sorting/discarding, passing on, reading, and passing on. Even with significant discarding or final disposition at each step of the process, 1000 letters can easily need to be handled 2000 times. (Some are handled once; others are handled four or five times.)

Contrast this with a disintermediated world in which e-mail messages come into the organization. The categorization is done not by clerks but by the authors before the messages arrive. (On a Web-based form, you may be asked to select the subject of your message. You cannot type in a subject: you must choose one for which the organization is prepared.)

With the messages in electronic form and categorized by their authors, no further sorting and scanning are required. Someone—even a CEO—can select the 1 or 10 or 100 messages that can be processed in the available time. Instead of the winnowing being done manually, it is done automatically so that the people with final authority process messages directly.

Obviously, there is a massive change in the organization. The clerks who open, scan, and sort messages are automated out of the picture. More senior people with authority to handle the messages proliferate. And the authors of messages should receive more prompt attention.

Life in the Digital World

The digital world includes people who are comfortable with the new technology; it also includes adaptations of traditional concepts to the wired world. Once such adaptation is digital branding—the integration of all media into a single brand or concept for an organization. This book explores many of these adaptations in detail.

Support for Bricks-and-Mortar Life

Finally, Web-based enterprises live in the real world. This is important to remember amidst the hoopla (and confusion!) of new technologies. There are people involved, there are locations from which those people transact business, and purely Web-based organizations are almost nonexistent. The interface between the bricks-and-mortar life and the virtual life on the Web is one of the issues explored in this book.

Concretization

Operations and activities—be they sales, queries, or other pursuits—can be described in abstract terms. When it comes to actually carrying them out, they are concretized in one way or another: an invoice is handwritten, a telephone call is made, or a Web form is transmitted. These activities remain relatively constant regardless of the methods or media used to carry them out. (A query as to the status of an order is essentially the same whether it is done face-to-face, over the telephone, or via e-mail.)

However, when the process is concretized in a virtual, Web-based way, it often is quite different from one that is concretized in the traditional form. Once concretized in either a virtual or Web-based form or in a traditional, bricks-and-mortar form, an activity often cannot easily be converted to the other form.

Whenever a process that has been concretized in one form meets a process that has been concretized in the other, problems can occur. (For example, online merchants have little trouble running their Web sites; however, processing returns—a set of transactions involving permissions, rebilling, and shipping—frequently is a stumbling block.) Sometimes there is no choice as to which form a process takes: chairs cannot be shipped over the Internet, they must be shipped in trucks.

Recognizing the points in your operations at which concretization choices are made is an essential part of developing a

Web-based enterprise. These are critical fault lines where problems frequently occur and where definitions, standards, and practices need to be clearly defined. It is easy to click the back arrow on your browser: there is no back arrow on a delivery truck.

The Growth and Development of Web-Based Enterprises

Web-based enterprises arise in any of three ways:

1. They can start as new enterprises—the now-legendary "dot.com" companies.

2. They can be deliberate additions to and evolutions of existing organizations.

3. They can be "skunk-works" projects that have sprung up inside organizations but outside formal management structures. These projects need to be merged with the rest of the organization's functions without unduly harming any of those functions (or the skunk-works project).

How a Web-based enterprise evolves often has a great deal to do with its later life: its problems, successes, and challenges.

Starting a Web-Based Enterprise

In some ways, starting from scratch is the easiest way to develop a Web-based enterprise. It certainly is the most exciting!

Why This Matters

The pitfall in such cases, though, is usually that the Web side of the enterprise is well developed and the other aspects are rudimentary. Personnel policies are needed; desks are needed—either in an office or in telecommuters' homes. Legacy systems (and legacy employees) are not issues in many cases; however, there is a very real danger of inventing from scratch basic organizational policies and procedures.

Adding Web-Based Activities to Your Company

This is the approach that many existing organizations choose. In many cases, there is no choice: you cannot disband the organization and start over from scratch just to put up a Web site.

Why This Matters

Here, the pitfall is likely to be a too-slavish reproduction of the original organization in the Web-based organization. The opportunity to question and reinvent the enterprise cannot be ignored.

Legacy systems and legacy employees can be stumbling blocks. The issues of loyalty and experience that are covered in later chapters come to the fore.

Taking Control of a Web-Based Enterprise

Perhaps the most challenging Web-based enterprise is the one that you wake up one morning and discover to have emerged from an informal project—perhaps one you never knew about. In these cases, corporate policy is likely to be made by webmasters and Web page designers who suddenly realize that they need two sentences explaining the organization's privacy statement—and then proceed to write them!

Why This Matters

Clearly, there are management issues involved in these ad hoc Web sites. You have to tread carefully, though. Frequently, these skunk-works projects have been wildly successful; often, the people who are happy to work long and hard hours on such projects are less than happy to work even regular hours on more structured projects. The transition is tricky: this book can help.

In most cases, you have no choice about how your Web-based enterprise has started to grow. No matter how your Web-based enterprise has grown and developed, the issues are the same: integrating the Web and non-Web aspects of the organization and avoiding conflicts, inconsistencies, and duplication.

What You Can Do About It

If your organization has any sort of Web presence or Internet access, it falls into one of these categories. If you are just starting out, you can choose how to proceed.

Organizational Origins of Web-Based Enterprises

Regardless of how a Web-based enterprise has evolved, its origins can be in any of several organizational entities. As with the growth and development of a Web-based enterprise, its organizational roots often influence its later existence.

The most common origins are:

- Computer/information technology
- Graphics, publications, and press relations
- Sales
- Individuals and skunk-works groups
- New entities

Unlike your lack of choice about the growth and development of a Web-based enterprise discussed in the previous section, you often do have control over the organizational origins of your Web presence.

If your organization is small, you may not have separate departments. In a one-person business, the owner does everything (or hires consultants as needed). Even in those cases, however, you have different aspects of your business. You know, for example, when you have your financial planning hat on and when you have your shipping clerk hat on.

Computer/ Information Technology

As an outgrowth of their traditional technology role, many computer and IT departments have implemented internal networks. They are often the people to hook up desktop computers to internal and external networks, and they frequently wind up placing servers on those networks (with or without direct guidance).

Why This Matters

When a Web presence grows from this area, it is often characterized by less than optimal interfaces. The performance of the network may be excellent, but sometimes users are asked to do things that are not always intuitive. The graphics often are borrowed and not great.

Over time, these origins for Web presences can pose difficulties if the organization is interested in moving servers and other equipment off site. The ownership issue can be a serious problem.

Graphics, Publications, and Press Relations

Web sites often arise from these areas of an organization as part of their standard operations.

Why This Matters

In these cases, the problems are often the reverse of those that occur when a Web presence arises from the technical side of an organization. The graphics and content are likely to be excellent. However, the technical support may be lacking. In many cases, the publications and press arms of an organization are used to contracting with outside vendors for printing and such services; they may have done so to set up their Web site. More than one organization has discovered that it had a Web site that it knows nothing about.

Integrating these sites with a corporate network can be difficult—both technically and from the personnel side. One common problem that arises is security. Whereas an IT staff is often quite sensitive to security issues, a press department rarely worries about security (except for the transient needs of embargoing documents until a stated release date). Their job is to get information out, and the notion that some information should not get out is anathema to many people.

Sales and Other Operations	Sometimes a Web site is set up by a sales operation or another part of the enterprise that needs to deal with the public.
Why This Matters	As with Web presences that arise from the graphics, publications, and press relations areas, these sites are often subcontracted. For example, a library may have its catalog placed on the Internet by the company that provides its catalog support. This is all well and good, but it tends to distort the presence in favor of the part of the enterprise that has seized the initiative.
Individuals and Skunk-Works Groups	The entrance barriers to Web publishing are so low that anyone can create and maintain a Web site. You may find one—or many—such sites within your organization. Sometimes they arise more or less formally ("my brother-in-law will put your Web page on his site if you want"); other times they are totally informal.
Why This Matters	These projects can be highly productive and motivating. Unfortunately, they can serve to point up the failings (and slowness) of organizational structures within the company. More than one organization has seen bright people put together a

Web site outside the corporate rules—and then leave to start their own company. If your organization can innovate only by going outside its management structures, you have bigger problems than a Web site.

It is not just the lack of control that can be a problem. For every company that finds junior assistants developing Web sites, another company finds its senior staff doing the same. In the first case, you may be getting a bargain by having junior staff do sophisticated Web design; in the second case, you may be paying far too much—and letting other operations go by the board.

An organization's Web presence and Internet operations need to be managed just as much as any other project needs to be managed.

New Entities

Some companies set up Web teams and Internet departments to handle the special needs of a Web-based enterprise.

Why This Matters

Web teams and Internet departments succeed when they are small support organizations. Too often, they become closed power centers surrounded by jargon and mystery.

In the long run, the only way to use the Internet successfully in an organization is to recognize that it will affect every part of the enterprise and to decentralize its management and control. (The Internet, after all, is perhaps the greatest example of a successful decentralized system that the world has every seen.)

The successful Web-based enterprise uses the Web and the Internet throughout its operations; they are not restricted or special technologies. By the same token, successful Web-based enterprises recognize that although many of the technologies of the Web are simple, expertise is required to use them to best advantage.

It is decidedly a good idea to have IT staff (consultants or in house) cable computers and set up addresses, but that in no way should be taken as an indication that their expertise automatically extends to putting up Web pages. By the same token, graphics professionals can put up Web pages, but they should not be expected—or even allowed—to do anything but the most rudimentary hardware support.

A small organization in which everyone does everything may mimic the excitement of start-up Internet companies—including the fact that they often do not make money at the beginning and their employees work for stock options (i.e., minimum wage).

| What You Can Do | Take charge of your organization's Web presence and Internet operations before they take charge of you. Identify where you are with regard to these basic paradigms and figure out how to move from there to a truly integrated operation in which everyone's talents are used to their best advantage. |

Summary

This chapter has presented the basic concepts of the book. Specifically, the idea of the Web-based enterprise has been discussed and defined, along with how Web-based enterprises grow and develop and where they come from within an organization.

The remaining chapters in this part of the book deal with how people use the Web, where people use the Web, and what you can do about all of this. The second part of the book focuses on Web sites and pages; the third part addresses staffing issues.

2

How People Use Computers and the Web

Old-timers on the Web remember the days when they knew almost every Web site. With the exponential growth of the Web, those days are long gone. It is hard for some people to believe it, but there are young children surfing the Web today who have never known a world without the World Wide Web. Among the young wired generation, terms like "Gopher" and "Veronica" are just as mysterious as they were to the nonwired population in the early 1990s.

This chapter is about how people use computers and the Web today. After several rapid years of wild growth and experimentation, Web standards (both formal and informal) have emerged. Those standards and terminology are also part of this chapter. These are not just abstract notions: understanding how people use computers and the Web is a critical step in developing and managing your Web-based enterprise. The Internet is littered with hundreds of sites that are designed backward—they present information in the way in which the author wants to present it rather than in the way in which people want to receive and use it.

- *"Models of Interaction"describes how people interact with Web pages and what their expectations are.*

- *"Purposes of Interaction"explores what it is that people do with Web pages.*

- *"The Web at Work and Play"concerns the blurring of lines on the Web. The differences between work and play, private and public, personal and professional are less clear than in the traditional world.*

- *"The Web and Other Tools"covers the other Internet tools: e-mail, file transfer protocol (FTP), and Telnet.*

- *"What You Can Do" shows you how to use the principles outlined in this chapter to develop and maintain your Web pages effectively.*

Models of Interaction

The Web is an interactive communications medium. It is similar to other such media in many ways, and it is different in a few. Marshall McLuhan may have gone a little far in writing that "the medium is the message," but it certainly is a large part of the message. People interact differently when they read paper-based documents and when they speak face to face. When they use the Web, they act differently again.

Writing and conversation are millennia-old human behaviors; using the Web is less than a decade old. However, it is scarcely surprising that it draws on the precedents of the other communications media. What is important to note here is that the ways in which people use these media are related to their expectations of those media. Expectations play a major role in communications. If you design a Web site that behaves the way a printed brochure does (or the way a streetcorner conversation does), you will likely confuse your visitors.

Writing

Writing is a time-honored communications medium with a variety of characteristics that matter in the Web age.

Individual

Communication is usually from one or more authors to an individual who is reading the document.

Permanence

Although paper is subject to decay (and loss) over time, most paper-based communication is not ephemeral. You can re-read the last paragraph or catch up on last week's newspaper.

Delay

There is a delay between writing and publication and reading.

Linear Logic

A premium is placed on logical development. Thousands of years of work have honed the principles of exposition and argument. Paper-based communication is often revised over and over before it is presented to its readers.

Conversation

Personal communication is usually face to face. It differs from written communication in a number of ways.

Groups

By definition, conversation includes at least two people; it is not an individual activity. Any number of people may be part of the conversation.

Ephemeral

Even if you ask someone to repeat what was just said, that request is likely to produce a different set of words. This is why minutes are taken at important meetings: they convert the ephemeral speech to the relatively permanent written record.

Instantaneous   The give and take of a conversation is immediate.

Spontaneous Logic   Personal communication is spontaneous; although it may have much of the logic of written communication, a verbatim transcript of a conversation often reveals surprising gaps that the participants blithely jump over because they understand what they are saying.

The Web   Electronic communication on the Web combines characteristics of both written communication and conversation.

Individual   There is usually a single reader of a Web page. Web browsing is normally not a collaborative experience.

Ephemeral and Permanent   It is both ephemeral and permanent—and the reader cannot tell in advance whether an individual Web page is of one sort or the other. The top story on an Internet news site may change from minute to minute; catching up on last week's news may be impossible because the story that appeared last week is now updated with more information. On the other hand, much Web content is quite out of date.

Because this aspect is ambiguous on the Web, you should do everything you can to let people know if the content they are viewing is likely to be there in the same format if they return.

Instantaneous   It is instantaneous (like conversations).

Nonlinear Logic   Unlike conversations, it is not spontaneous. The well-reasoned arguments that people are used to in print are relevant on the Web; the gaps of normal conversations are simply mysterious on the Web.

However, it is important to note that the logic and rhetoric of the Web are quite different from those of paper. This is in part because of the Web's hypertext base. Whereas paper-based arguments are of necessity linear, Web-based arguments are not.

Why This Matters

Understanding that the Web is a new medium that has characteristics in common with other media makes your job much easier as you approach a Web site. Many people start from scratch, ignoring the past or reinventing it.

Those aspects of Web pages that are rooted in print communications can be studied by referring to the classic references for print: references on design, rhetoric, and style. Those aspects that derive from characteristics of personal communications can be researched with works on sociology, psychology, advertising, and other means of persuasion. Focus on the aspects of the Web that are unique to this medium in your research and analysis.

What You Can Do

Whether yours is a one-person organization or a global enterprise, the message of this book is the same: integrate the Web as seamlessly as possible into your operations. As you have seen in this section, the Web has characteristics in common with other communications tools that you probably use and in which you have developed corporate expertise.

The people who write your corporate documents may be new to the Web, but they are not new to language. By clarifying for them what aspects of print media apply to the Web and which ones do not, you can rely on and further develop their skills and experience.

You may need to do this on a case-by-case basis. Some of your staff may be afraid of the Web (and afraid that their jobs will disappear). Others may be temperamentally inclined to drop all their "old-fashioned" work and launch themselves precipitously onto the Web.

Purposes of Interaction

The models of interaction described in the last section apply to many activities. What people actually do in their interaction is the topic of this section.

Life on the Web falls into two general categories: shopping and browsing. This is scarcely surprising to old hands in the computer world: decades ago all computer operations were evenly divided into transaction processing (similar to shopping) and research and analysis. Although there are borderline cases, the extent to which this dichotomy remains and is useful in viewing the Web is remarkable.

Shopping and Transactions

Shopping and transaction processing are the heartbeat of e-commerce. They are characterized by the fact that items of value change hands. That characteristic leads to a whole host of issues that need to be addressed.

Security

Transactions often need secure surroundings. This is true in the real world, too: banks keep their money in steel vaults, not cardboard boxes.

Security consists not just of safeguarding valuable items but also of identifying people properly. In the real world, your signature is used on documents not only to signify that you approve but also in order to identify you.

Both of these aspects of security—safekeeping and identification—are critical on the Web. In fact, they can pose particular challenges on the Web.

History and Reproducibility

Transactions need to be recorded. Note that this is a characteristic of paper-based transactions; it is not always characteristic of electronic transactions. Not only do transactions need to be recorded, but that record needs to remain intact.

This requirement often stands in contrast to other needs. For example, the price of a pair of shoes that you ordered last week must remain the price as it was last week for purposes of your invoice. The price of those shoes today may be different, and that price needs to be reflected on the pages advertising items in the store.

Commitment

Transactions are characterized by a single moment of **commitment**: the moment at which all parts of the transaction are deemed to occur. In shopping (on line and in the real world), this is the moment when you hand over the money or your credit card. Until that moment, you can return items to the shelf or add new items. After that moment, the inventory lists are updated and returning items has to be done in a more formal way.

Browsing, Searching, and Surfing

Standing beside transactions you find all other activities on the Web. In Web terms, these consist of browsing, searching, and surfing, but they correspond to the general concept of research and analysis that many companies identified years ago. Their common thread is that they are all involved with publicly available information (if the information is sold, then you have an exchange of value and you are technically dealing with a transaction).

In just about every regard, these activities are differentiated from transactions.

Public Availability

When it comes to information uses of the Web, security plays a much different role. A vast amount of the Web's information is simply not secure: if you are opening an e-commerce business, you want people all over the world to be able to access your site.

As the Web grows, many people are trying to convert the free information to pay-for-use information. This is not just a matter of asking for a credit card number; it is a matter of converting an informational site to a transactional site.

One aspect of security that is relevant on informational Web sites is that of privacy—the browser's privacy. Technology allows you to collect a great deal of information on the people who use your site. In some places, this data collection is regulated very tightly. In others, it is not. Privacy policies should be clearly posted so that people know what you are collecting.

Changeable Information

As a general rule, people want the latest and most complete information when they are surfing the Web. Thus, rather than being careful to be able to preserve what someone saw on your site last week, you need to devote your efforts to making the data up to date.

Browsing and Surfing

As people look for information, they come and go (just as they do on a shopping street). There is no moment of commitment as there is in a transactional world; in fact, there is nothing comparable to a transaction. You often find yourself starting to do one thing and actually doing another.

Measuring Success and Failure of Interactions

When you identify the goals people have when they access your Web pages, you are in a position to measure the success or failure of those pages. This is critical in developing a useful site.

Step one is to determine—often on a page-by-page basis—whether a page is transactional in nature or informational. The second step is to set up some way of defining goals and measuring your success at achieving them.

From the User's Point of View

From the user's point of view, it is fairly easy to decide whether a page is useful. Does it have what you want (the information, the goods you want to buy)? Can you find what you want? Was it easy to do so?

Unfortunately, gathering this data directly is at least partly counterproductive. Asking someone to respond to a question such as "Did this page answer your needs?" adds a degree of complexity to the page. It may take only a few moments to read the question and a mouse click to answer it, but it requires back-end programming (to collect and collate the data), the question itself takes up space on the page, and it draws attention to the medium rather than to the content (which, presumably, is what the user is interested in).

You can gather data indirectly, though. Uncompleted transactions (abandoned shopping carts) are a sign of some kind of trouble. On informational sites, it is sometimes less clear, but you can certainly track phone calls and e-mail from people asking questions that are answered on your site—and that they could not find for themselves.

What is critical is to remember that in almost all cases, you should be keeping your users in mind. You must understand their expectations, know what they want from your site (which is largely a function of what you have led them to believe they will find there), and find ways to track their behavior without infringing on their privacy.

The cases in which you do not care about users are those in which your publication of information is done to satisfy a formal requirement. In the non-wired world, such postings as marriage banns play a similar role. They must be posted, but it is not your responsibility to make certain that anyone sees them.

From the Provider's Point of View

If you establish goals for yourself, you should be able to track the success of your Web pages. (If you do not establish goals and objectives for yourself, you are skipping a critical management step.)

The most basic tracking that you can do is the number of hits to your site; you can (subject to privacy considerations) track where those hits come from. Beyond that, you can track completed transactions and the (inferred) success of information searches. In the latter case, a reduction in telephone or e-mail queries or anecdotal reports of people finding information on your Web site can be useful.

Compare the tracking that you do from the user's point of view with that done from your point of view. Tracking from the user's point of view often involves the failures of your site—the abandoned shopping cart or the phone call to ask a question. Tracking from your point of view often involves successes—congratulatory messages or sales. This situation exists simply because it is usually easier to track the information in this way.

Why This Matters

Categorizing each of your Web pages as transactional or informational can be critically useful to you. Often, the transactional pages are hosted on a separate server—or outsourced to an e-commerce company.

Issues of design and maintenance are also critical here. Remember that transactions always involve the exchange of value: the Web equivalent of bonded employees should work on those pages. It is remarkable just how lax security on the Web often is.

The Web at Work and Play

Like other communications media, the Web can be used for work and play, public or private activities, and in ways that combine these. If you can make a distinction for your site, do so. Anything that clarifies your intentions makes it easier for people to understand the expectations that they should have.

Because people can move seamlessly from page to page, it is sometimes hard to categorize their behavior in traditional ways. The subliminal cues such as clothing or tone of voice that help distinguish between work and play and between public and private lives are missing on the Web. Additionally, the barriers between such spaces are missing so people are not aware of passing from an e-commerce shop to a newspaper.

Why This Matters

As a result, you may have to deal with some issues that surprise you. Many people expect there to be no barriers on the Web, and you may find your employees, customers, or vendors expecting to have their own space on your Web site—or at least links to their own sites. This will happen, and it is best to decide what you are going to do about it before a crisis emerges.

The Web and Other Tools

The Web is just one of the Internet tools that people use today. A few years ago, it was very simple to list the Internet protocols: they consisted of the Web, e-mail, file transfer, Usenet news, and Telnet. Today, it is not so simple. You can use the Web for e-mail or news. Telnet is rapidly fading from view as legacy systems opt for Web interfaces, and Web-based file transfer is supplanting FTP for many users.

Nevertheless, the other Internet protocols remain alive and well. The major ones are identified here.

E-Mail

The basic Internet e-mail protocols are designed for sending and receiving mail. Simple Mail Transfer Protocol (SMTP) is used to send mail. Receiving mail is done with a variety of protocols including Post Office Protocol (POP) and Internet Mail Access Protocol (IMAP).

E-mail services normally come with Internet access. Packages for small business often include several e-mail accounts and software that allows you to maintain them. If you have your own domain name, mail to any address at that domain is delivered to a single computer. Most Internet service providers allow you to maintain forwarding addresses so that your staff need not have their own e-mail on the same computer. In other words, mail addressed to info@yourdomain.com is automatically forwarded to you@anotherlocation.net.

What You Can Do

In setting up such an operation, you should make certain that you have the ability to set up forwarding addresses. If it has to be done by your Internet service provider, a fee may be required and there may be delays.

Note, too, that once again the distinction between personal and private lives needs to be addressed. Forwarding mail to an employee's private mail account may be convenient, but it may cause problems in the future.

FTP	File transfer protocol (FTP) is one of the oldest Internet protocols; it is used to transfer files from one computer to another. Its commands are very basic and it is quite robust.
Why This Matters	You can request files be transferred using Web protocols. What matters is that when you transfer a file using a Web protocol, your browser will use its suffix (such as .txt, .html, or .pdf) to determine what application—if any—should be used to process the file on receipt. With FTP, you normally do nothing more than transfer the file. Thus, if you want to download documentation in Portable Document Format (PDF), you can do so with your browser and read the document right in the browser's window. Alternatively, you can download it with FTP, save the file, and read it later.
Telnet	Telnet uses the Internet's connectivity to let your personal computer function as if it were a dumb terminal connected to a computer. It is normally used for legacy applications. Over time, many of these legacy applications are falling into disuse; others are revised to allow more modern (usually Web-based) access.

What You Can Do

This chapter has described how people use the Web and computers today. Your job is to integrate that information into your plans for your Web-based enterprise and for its Web sites and pages.

Models of Interaction

For example, use the analysis in "Models of Interaction" starting on page 22 to decide whether individual Web pages should be clearly identified as permanent or ephemeral. Recognize that the logic that may have applied to a printed brochure may not apply to a Web site.

It is very tempting to try to transfer the linear logic of printed materials to a Web site. You will often find such sites on the Web. They are recognizable by their regimentation and insistence that you proceed from page one to page two and then on to page three. Unfortunately, this paradigm is very un-Web-like. People are used to viewing individual pages in context that they create through their clicking and surfing. Requiring someone to follow your personal navigation strategy is generally not a good idea on the Web.

When you do need to enforce a navigation strategy or to use linear logic on the Web, you can do so by integrating other media. For example, your Web pages can contain audio or video clips; by their nature, they are linear. Additionally, you can incorporate links to documents, either as text files, word processing documents, or (ideally) PDF files. The appearance of documents in a formatted fashion reminds people that they are in the world of linear logic and traditional writing.

Purposes of Interaction

Identify the purpose of your Web pages as discussed in "Purposes of Interaction" starting on page 26. If you are confronted with a Web page that appears to straddle the fence, consider rethinking it so that it is either transactional or informational. If you are uncertain about the purpose of a page, your users will likely also be uncertain.

The Web at Work and Play

Consider the issues raised in "The Web at Work and Play" starting on page 31 as you decide on the approach you take to each Web page and its content. Is it designed to be fun or is it deadly serious?

The issues involving privacy are even more interesting—and dangerous. Do you want to post photos of your employees? Should they have their own Web sites? What about links to sites that they recommend?

The Web and Other Tools

Finally, remember that the Web is only one of the Internet tools available today (see "The Web and Other Tools" starting on page 31). Not everything belongs on the Web. Remember that forcing people to use Web-based e-mail may exclude some people for whom that form of e-mail is not available.

Summary

It is important to note the ways in which the Web is like traditional written and verbal communication and the ways in which it is different. Understanding the similarities lets you take advantage of millennia of work aimed at clarifying communication. Realizing the differences helps you avoid blind alleys as you attempt to do things that will not work on the Web.

This chapter has focused on how people use the Web; the principles apply to just about every page on the Web. The next chapter focuses on where people use the Web; its emphasis is on Web sites rather than individual pages.

3

Web Places, Security, and Privacy

In the previous chapter, you saw how people use computers and the Web. The focus of that chapter was on the interaction between people and computers: the nature of those interactions compared with written and conversational communication, the purposes of those interactions (transactional and informational), the lack of boundaries between public and private life and between work and play, and how other tools are used to augment the Web.

In this chapter, the emphasis is on the places where people use the Web and on how they relate to Web sites (as opposed to individual pages—the focus of the previous chapter). Like the previous chapter, this addresses issues larger than how to design individual pages and what to put on your site. For many people, those questions are the beginning and ending of their Web site analysis. Unfortunately, their sites show this lack of analysis.

- *In "Places of Interaction" you will see how a Web sites's scope defines the interaction that it can support.*

- *"Security" addresses the critical issue of the security that you must provide for yourself, your Web site, and your users. (As you know from your own life off the Web, a sense of security is almost always connected with a specific place. For that reason, security is discussed in this chapter along with Web places.)*

- *Closely allied to security, the issue of privacy is increasingly important. It is covered in the section called "Privacy."[1]*

Places of Interaction

You cannot take a picture of the Internet or the Web: for all the talk about "being on the Web," the place under discussion does not exist. However, that does not mean that Web places do not exist. In fact, when people are using the Web, they are dealing simultaneously with four places:

1. The first place is where the user actually is at the time. This may be home or office; it may involve a desktop or laptop computer, a television set-top box, a wireless device such as a telephone or handheld organizer, or other Internet access devices now being devised.

2. The second place involved in Web access is the place where the Web server is located. The Web server is the device that responds to the request to transmit a page such as http://www.yourdomain.com/info.html.

---

1. See Chapter 15, "Security," in *Database-Driven Web Sites* for more details on cookies and passwords.

3. The third place is where the site owner is located.

4. The fourth place is the virtual place that the user imagines.

Where Is the User?

At first glance, you may think this is not your concern: as long as someone is using your Web site, all is well and good. Think again. This issue is precisely the one that you need to consider when you decide exactly how you will use the Web within your organization.

For organizations with an intranet or an extranet (an intranet accessible from the outside with proper identification), you may know where your users are. You may well have a range of options, since you can determine which pages on your site (or sites) will be available to which types of users and to which specific locations.

Your choices are rarely as easy as they seem. One of the biggest that you will encounter is what to do about telecommuters and people working from home. In short, is your workplace confined to your office or does it encompass hotel rooms, individuals' homes, and consultants' offices?

What You Can Do

Decide first of all if you want to limit access to pages on your site by the location of users. (Limiting access by the identity of users is discussed later in this chapter in "Security" starting on page 46.) These limitations can be in either direction: you can restrict some pages to access from the inside (whatever "inside" means in your environment), and you can restrict some pages to access from the outside. In the second case, for instance, you may wish to prevent access to public information about your company; doing so would force employees and other authorized users to use private and more complete information. Such a strategy can prevent confusion and phone calls to a human resources office from people who have not found the information that they want on the public pages but who are entitled to that information.

Where Is the Web Server?

For an individual user, only the first location (where the user is) is clear. The following example shows why. Figure 3-1 is a typical home page. It is the home page of Philmont Software Mill (the author's consulting company).

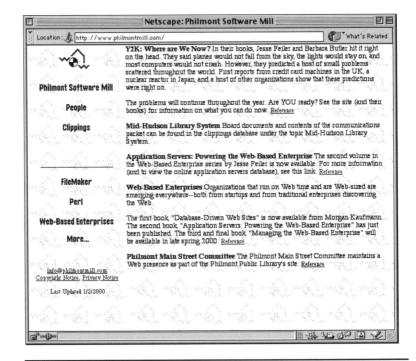

FIGURE 3-1. Philmont Software Mill Home Page

The page is created using frames, a technology that allows a single Web page to contain two separate Web pages. (For more information on frames, see "Composite Pages (Frames)" starting on page 137.) The left-hand side of the screen consists of navigation buttons (Philmont Software Mill, People, Clippings, and so forth). It is a Web page that is hosted on a computer in Chatham, New York. On the right, dynamic content is presented from a page built on the fly by a Web server in Bothell, Washington that runs FileMaker Pro. The distance between the two Web servers is approximately 2368 miles (3810 km).

Thus, it would appear that the page is composed of elements from two Web servers. However, this is not necessarily the case. The frame at the left is relatively unchangeable. As a result, it can be cached for performance reasons in a variety of places: the user's browser cache, the user's Internet service provider's cache, or in various caches located at various nodes in the Internet (such caches are created to improve performance).

Although the law is not yet clear in this area, there appears to be a general sense that a cache in an Internet service provider's installation is not the same as the original Web server. Generally, the Internet service provider caches pages without regard to their content, although the frequency of their use does often affect decisions on caching. So even though a page—or part of a page—may actually come from a cache somewhere on the user's machine or on the Internet, that source is not considered in the same regard as the original location of the Web server. This poses a very interesting problem in cases where the original server disappears or goes off line and only the cached copies remain.

Note that the location of the Web server is relevant to individual pages on a site. Sites can be composed of pages from a variety of sources, and—as Figure 3-1 demonstrates—a single apparent page may consist of several actual pages.

Why This Matters   There are three issues in which the physical location of the Web server matters:

1. Taxation and regulation

2. Performance

3. Maintenance

Taxation and Regulation   Certain activities (particularly gambling and pornography) are regulated and even banned in some locations. A Web server that supports such activities thus needs to abide by the laws of that location.

Before you dismiss this issue on the grounds that you do not carry out such activities on your site, note that other laws and regulations apply to Web sites. One of the most important areas is that of privacy (see "Privacy" starting on page 59 later in this chapter). As of this writing, the laws of the European community are significantly tougher than those of the United States.

Although performance caches in Web servers are not generally considered in the same way that original Web servers are, mirror sites deliberately set up by an organization typically are considered as original Web servers. Thus, if a U.S. company locates its Web pages on servers in Europe, the United States, and Asia, those pages may fall under different regulatory rules with regard to issues such as privacy.

Since this issue is in a state of flux, the most that you can do is to be aware of it and to consider which—if any—of your site's pages should be placed on mirrored sites around the world. Do not assume that sites are transportable.

Performance   The physical location of the site can have a significant impact on performance. Within a corporate intranet, a Web site that is located on a server across the hall can be much more responsive than one halfway around the world. On the other hand, a corporate Web site on an intranet that contains critical corporate information may be located on a low-powered server and may be so overwhelmed with Internet traffic that its performance is far worse than that of a major Web site on the other side of the world.

If you can control the location of the site vis-à-vis the location of your site's users, you can optimize performance. Such control is typically greatest on intranets and other tightly controlled networks. It also comes into play for local businesses most of whose customers are in one region.

Maintenance   Finally, the locations of the Web server and of caches matter because changes that you make may take some time to be reflected on users' browsers. Even the original Web server may have a cache, and an uploaded page on your site may not be served out for a period of time. It may seem strange to you, but it is not uncommon for a period of days to elapse before a Web site is updated throughout the world.

Once again, knowing your users and their behavior will help you out. If they are business users who access your site during the week, consider updating the site on a Friday night—giving caches around the world the weekend to be updated.

Of course, for large organizations that control their own caches around the world, the issue of updates is more manageable since they can frequently control when new pages are available for download. However, even in those cases, there is no way of controlling what appears on a user's computer. If a computer in the display of a retail store displays a Web site when the store closes at the end of Friday, that same Web site—un-updated—may well appear in the display on Monday morning.

Where Is the Site Owner?

The next question—where is the site owner?—is sometimes fairly easy to answer. Somewhere on the site (usually) is identification of the proprietor. In fact, generally accepted privacy standards require that a physical mailing address be provided for the site owner so that questions regarding privacy can be addressed without using a possibly unsafe Internet connection. (In the case of the site described here, the company owning it is located in Philmont, NY—8 miles (13 km) from Chatham.)

Generally, the location of the site owner carries great legal weight when it comes to issues of taxation and regulation. However, not every page carries identification. If you doubt this, use an Internet search engine to search for any technical term. You will probably find a number of pages prepared by consultants, students, and others, describing the term or presenting papers and presentations on the term. Some of those pages may be signed; others may have been intended to be viewed by traversing a link from a home page—but the search engine has bypassed that link and plunged you right into the middle of the now-unidentified site.

What You Can Do

There is no requirement that each page be identified, and because of the variety of descriptive information that may be required, many Web page designers are loath to add such descriptions. Remember that users are not required to follow your path of navigation, and so they may easily land on unidentified pages. The answer is simple: either add the identification to all pages or add a single link to all pages; the link can then refer back to a site-wide page with privacy, security, and copyright information.

One way of forcing the user to have seen identifying information is to use dynamically created Web pages. In such cases, the user most stop at a preliminary page to formulate a request. (This can be done explicitly or with a button that contains form or scripted parameters to cause a dynamic page to be created.) Be careful, though: adept users may be able to bypass this mechanism and create the queries for themselves.

What Is the Virtual Web Site Place?

Finally, there is another place involved in Web browsing—the virtual place that you create for your site and its pages. This is the place that people refer to when they talk about your site. Remember that on the Web there are no visual cues to the size of an organization as there are in the real world. However, there is an increasing number of Web cues that help identify the environment of a Web site. A background of yellow smiley faces portrays quite a different set of cues than does a background of yellow tulips or of lined yellow paper. (And a site whose backgrounds change from one to the other of these conveys a different sense than a site with a common background.)

Beyond the graphics, the style of the text and the arrangement of the content contribute to a site's sense of place.

What You Can Do

Use backgrounds and layouts of pages on your site to help people know what belongs together and what is separate. (See "Designing the Pages" starting on page 233 for more on this topic.)

Try to decide what you want to convey by way of place. Metaphors from the world of architecture can be very useful here; useful, too, are abstract metaphors from the worlds of art and design. Here are some ideas of place that you may want to consider:

- How many places will you have on your site? This is totally separate from the number and location of your Web servers: they reflect the implementation of your strategy, not its visible characteristics.

- Do you want an internal area? If so, users should know that they are behind an invisible wall and that they are not observed by the public. Conversations can be informal and can contain private information. You need a multitude of cues to remind people that they are in such a private area.

- Do you need separate areas for different types of visitors—tourists, browsers, clients, and prospective employees? (Too many areas make your site confusing and people lose the sense of knowing where they are.)

- Is your site kid-friendly or adults only? (Do not think this just has to do with sex and violence: it also has to do with the style of text and graphics as well as the content. A science site geared for kids is quite different from one geared to interested laypeople—and in turn it is quite different from one aimed at postgraduate science professors.

- Do you want to make separate areas for different types of connections or browsers? In some cases, pages with streaming video can be presented only to users with high-speed Internet access. You can create a parallel universe for such users, or you can just provide options on pages that otherwise are undifferentiated. (The classic frames/no frames sites are examples of this.)

- Another classic—text-only sites—also by default creates separate senses of place.

- Finally, consider whether your site's sense of place should match or mirror another site's places (subject to copyright constraints, of course). A consortium of organizations can in this way create a place that appears bigger than each individual site.

Security

Security is safety and the sense of freedom from danger. Security is one of the attributes of places both real and virtual. In view of the fact that you are dealing with at least four different places (the location of the user, the location of the Web server, the location of the Web owner, and the virtual location of the site), security is an important concern. Each of the places involved has its own degree of security whether you attend to it or not. Ignoring security issues does not make them go away: it means simply that you use someone else's security implementation.

Security on the Web consists of three issues:

1. **Authentication**: Are you certain you know who you are dealing with?

2. **Access**: Is the place you are using safe from intruders; are the information and other valuables located there safe from theft and corruption?

3. **Transmission**: Are your communications from one place to another secure?

Authentication

Knowing who you are dealing with matters both to users and to site administrators. For the user, authentication consists of knowing that www.yourbusiness.com really is the site that belongs to your business. For the site administrator, of course, authentication means that—when it matters—you know that Graciela WebBrowser really is who she says she is.

Authentication is accomplished in any of three ways:

1. A **trusted third party** can be used to assure the identity of one or both parties to a transaction.

2. **Passwords** or other mutually agreed-on codes can be exchanged directly between the two parties.

3. Authentication can also be accomplished by **identification**.

Any of these techniques can be used; in some cases they can be combined. Each of them has close parallels in the noncomputer world.

Note that authenticating a user's identity may or may not be necessary. If you are running a site that is not open to the public, you must know that the people using it are legitimate users. However, for the vast majority of informational sites, the identity of the user matters only when a transaction needs to occur. Deciding when and how to authenticate your users is part of the general issue of authentication.

Why This Matters

A user may want to make certain that a specific site is authentic, and a site may need to know that a supposed user is in fact that user. Thus, you may need to authenticate your users as well as yourself. For internal Web sites, authentication is critical to avoid releasing private information to the public.

Trusted Third Parties

A common form of authentication is the use of trusted third parties. This is the method used throughout the world for passport identification. An individual provides proof of identity to a government agency. If satisfied, that agency then produces a passport which stakes the government's credibility on the identity of the individual. When you try to enter another country, you do not have to present individual forms of identification: your government's documentation—your passport—suffices.

Note that the use of a trusted third party requires that the two parties involved agree on such a party. As is obvious from reports of negotiations of all sorts, such an agreement can often be contentious. In the case of passports, there is general agreement. However, when it comes to authentication on the Internet, a variety of vendors offer to provide such services.

You probably use a form of trusted third party authentication on a routine basis. If you search for information on the Web, you may rely on a search engine such as Yahoo! to find pages and sites for you. You trust Yahoo! and rely—to a greater or lesser extent—on its recommendations and on the fact that they are, indeed, what they purport to be. For many people, a higher level of certainty is provided by direct links from newspaper articles and other media. For example, earlier in this chapter, a reference was made to the author's Web site at www.philmontmill.com. You have every reason to believe that that reference is authentic.

What This Means to You   If your Web site is public, be generous with its address. Put it on your stationery, business cards, trucks, and letterhead. Make every attempt to include it in third party descriptions of your organization: someone reading a newspaper article can then be certain of finding you. In addition, you may want to make certain aggressively that people know where you are. This may involve advertising on sites that your customers and patrons trust.

For authentication of your users, you may want to require them to register with a trusted third party so that each transaction can be verified. This is done routinely for transactions involving money.

Passwords, Keys, and Codes   Passwords, keys, and codes do not require a third party. The two parties involved agree on a password or other identifier that represents their agreement as to one another's identity. (When you register for a Web site, you often provide such information.)

This is an improvement over third parties; however, it begs the question of how the authentication is handled in the first place. For many transactions, that authentication is handled in some other venue. For example, if you open a bank account, you may need to provide identification to the bank officer. At that time, you and the bank officer are certain of one another's identity: you are in the bank, and the officer is perusing your ID. You can then be issued a password which will be used in the online world.

Problems with Passwords, Keys, and Codes Passwords, keys, and codes all function in this way, and they all suffer from the same drawback: they can be mislaid or stolen. Someone who has a password (or user-ID/password combination) has the authentication mechanism to represent another person. The other party has no way of knowing about this misrepresentation.

The standard way around this is to remind people to safeguard these passwords. In addition, people are reminded to change passwords on a routine basis. Unfortunately, most individuals now have such a plethora of passwords, keys, and codes that they cannot remember them all, much less worry about changing them. People are writing down these passwords rather than committing them to memory—and as soon as they are written down, they are vulnerable to theft.

If you require people to register to use your Web site, you are potentially part of this problem. You need to store the passwords in a secure manner—encrypted, if at all possible. Herein lies yet another pitfall. You can generate passwords for people or you can ask them to choose passwords that they can remember. If you opt for the second choice, people will probably reuse passwords that they have used before (mother's maiden name, gemstone for their birth month, favorite wine, and so forth). If you store these passwords unencrypted, you may well store passwords to people's bank accounts and other personal information—simply because they have reused their passwords.

What You Can Do Do not store unencrypted passwords—particularly if users can choose them for themselves. If you must store unencrypted passwords, make certain that you have generated them.

Identification

Trusted third party authentication requires three parties; passwords, keys, and codes require two parties to agree. Identification can be done by a single party—often without the knowledge of the entity being authenticated. People do it all the time in life: "It's the cafe with the red awning just down the hill from the park." As in life, identification as a form of authentication relies on the completeness and accuracy of the information. If there are two cafes with red awnings just down the hill from the park, the lovers may never meet.

In many cases, identification is as simple as asking for someone's name. Although this is not particularly secure, it does provide a basic form of authentification. When you add a password to the identification (as is normally the case), you have a more secure means of authentication.

Identification frequently comes from a third party (as in the case of the directions to the cafe). This differs from the use of a trusted third party for authentication because that process involves the third party vouching for each party's identity. Simply providing information for you to use in later identifying an entity is a much different matter.

The main problem with the use of identification for authentication is that you do not know in advance if the identification will be unique. Names are not unique; identity numbers generally are, but they are not always satisfactory because some people have two or more. (This is often legitimate: a small-business owner may have a personal identifier and one for the business.)

The End of Authentication

All of the security in the world will not help your authentication process if you do not plan in advance how to terminate the authentication. This is a very serious problem for computer users. If you have logged into the most secure system and then decide to get up, leaving your computer still logged on, you have just handed someone your authenticated identity. As with the problem of writing down passwords, everyone knows not to do this—and people do it from time to time.

Furthermore, all types of authentication are obstacles to the smooth completion of transactions. The fact that they are necessary and are designed to be obstacles does not detract from this. One way of getting around this is to store the authentication information on a user's computer—often in a Web browser's cookie.

This is essentially the same as leaving the computer unattended. Anyone who uses your computer then has access to your authenticated identities as stored in cookies.

What You Can Do

One way to minimize (but not eliminate) the problem is to perform authentication for as brief a period as possible. On an e-commerce site, a rather informal form of authentication can be used for visitors who are browsing (this can be the entry of a name or the retrieval of a name from a cookie). When the transaction is about to be consummated, you can then require better authentication (perhaps with a password) for the one page on which the user enters a credit card number and clicks OK.

With regard to the use of cookies, avoid storing unencrypted information and particularly password information in them.

Access

The second aspect of security that you need to think about is access to the places involved in your Web site. You can control access with traditional bricks-and-mortar techniques, with implicit access controls, or with explicit access controls.

Bricks-and-Mortar Security

This is the most basic form of access control: bank vaults for centuries have provided this kind of access control. You simply place your computer in an area that is not accessible to people who should not be there.

This is the idea behind intranet security: if there is no physical connection to the Internet, unauthorized users cannot get in from the outside. Of course, within your organization you may still need to implement access controls for different people.

Implicit Access Controls

You can control access based on characteristics of the requests that are processed on your site. You can limit access to users with specific brands or versions of browsers; you can also limit access to people who are logging on from specific Internet addresses (IP addresses). You can limit access in the other direction as well: you can control the Internet addresses to which people within your organization can connect.

This type of access control is implicit in the sense that it is handled without the user knowing about it. The implementation is done using firewalls, proxy servers, or customized code.

Firewalls These are actually computers that implement this type of security. You can limit incoming or outgoing traffic to specific IP addressees or classes of IP addresses. Modern firewalls allow you to implement a vast array of such conditions. Many networking professionals have a well-deserved loathing of firewalls: it is very easy to lock legitimate users out. Try to make your security access rules as simple as possible to avoid such problems.

Proxy Servers These computers forward requests from individual users to Web sites as needed. Proxy servers often cache Web pages and are able to serve them up without actually accessing the Web. When they do pass a request along to the Web, they generally use their own address rather than that of the user. When the page is returned, the proxy server redirects it to the user who requested it.

This mechanism not only improves performance (through caching), it also simplifies the type of security in which an organization's access to a remote site such as a database needs to be from a predefined IP address. The address of the proxy server is that address.

Note that proxy servers and firewalls are often combined into a single unit.

Customized Code Many Web pages do their own testing for browser versions, IP addresses, and the like.

Explicit Access Controls

Implicit access controls use characteristics of the user's browser or address to manage access. Explicit access controls require the user to do something—such as enter a code. They can be implemented via a firewall or with customized code.

The code used for explicit access is not the same as a password, although it may appear similar. The purpose of a user ID and password is to authenticate someone's identity—that is, the identity of a single person. The purpose of a code used for explicit access control is to show that the person requesting access is one of the (possibly many) people allowed to access the resource.

Transmission

No matter how secure each computer and user's location is, the links among them represent potential security problems. This is the simplest aspect of security for many people to think about; it is also the simplest to handle—and often the least serious problem.

Because Internet communications are transmitted in packets, it is hard to tap a data communications line in the same way that a voice telephone line can be tapped. However, since messages are typically stored in many places (caches for Web pages, archives for e-mail messages), it is those stored messages that are vulnerable to theft and interception.

You have two concerns here:

1. If you store Web pages, e-mail messages, or other Internet traffic, you may become the possessor of valuable information. Many a computer has been stolen out of an office not for its intrinsic value but because it contains a file with passwords, credit card information, or other data of value.

2. Your data may wind up being stored in insecure locations from which it can be stolen.

Safeguarding Data Stores You Control

As noted previously, the simplest form of security is bricks and mortar (or steel). Your Web servers need to be located in places that keep them out of the way of people who have no business touching them. Remember that your Web servers are not just the computers hosting your site; as described in "Proxy Servers" on page 53, machines that you think are just designed to improve network performance may wind up containing valuable information of which you are unaware.

Safeguarding these data stores includes making certain that electronic access to them is safeguarded. It also means guaranteeing that regular backups are made and that those backups themselves are safeguarded with the same care afforded the original data.

This is all so obvious that you may wonder why it is even worth mentioning. Try performing a mental audit of the computers in your organization and in other organizations to which you have access. Which of them have data on them that you should not be able to access? And to which of those machines do you actually have access?

Safeguarding Your Data in Other Locations

Any data that is valuable to you should be kept safe. That means not allowing it to be stored in any location where it may be vulnerable to unauthorized use. And, as noted several times in this chapter, you must consider all intermediate caches on Web servers and in user browsers to be destinations that need to be secured.

The simplest way to safeguard data is to encrypt it using one of the many encryption techniques on the market today. For the vast majority of data, that type of simple encryption is just fine. Although an expert can decrypt much data, the effort is normally not worth it. (Many thefts of data are crimes of opportunity.)

What You Can Do

The three aspects of security (authentication, access, and transmission) all come into play once you have determined the level of security needed for data. While the most common failing here is to ignore security totally, the second most common failing is surely the blind implementation of security.

Here is what you need to do. It is both necessary and sufficient.

1. Identify what needs to be secured.

2. Identify the level of security.

3. Identify the owner.

Identify What Needs to Be Secured

You do not want to drive yourself, your colleagues, and your customers crazy with security, but you do need to systematically keep track of every item that needs to be secured. Identifying the secure items can be an endless task, comparable to the enormous unfinished corporate data dictionary projects of the 1980s. Here is how to do it and get on with your life.

Each object that will be secured will have a given level of security and an owner (these are described in the next two sections). Working backward, you can see that you must be able to define a secured object in such a way that it—and all of the data it contains—can fit into this paradigm.

For example, the source code for a Web page can be described in simple terms (the corporate telephone directory page, for example), its security can be stated simply (visible to all, updatable only by someone from the internal communications department), and its owner can be identified (the vice president of operations, perhaps).

If you define the secured object too finely—each telephone extension, for example—you may find yourself building an unsupportable edifice. If you define the secured object too grossly—all corporate information, for example—you may be unable to find a unique owner or to simply state the security level. If you encounter either problem (too much effort at developing and maintaining security or ambiguity in setting security attributes), rethink your definition of the secured object.

All of your information—data, Web pages, and so forth—needs to be covered by security. Secured items need not be of the same size: you can probably set the security attributes for everything within a corporate strategic planning division in one fell swoop (totally private, unpublishable in any media), while Web pages on your various sites may need to be handled on a department-by-department or even individual basis.

You may not have worried about security in the past; however, as soon as you are living in the Web-based world, several hundred million people have some sort of access to your information, and you need to know how to handle requests (both formal and hacker).

Identify the Level of Security

Again, do not be too particular about setting up a complex system of security levels. Security levels are actually pairs of data: a level and the entity (or entities) to which it applies. For a given secured object, any number of these pairs may exist.

A simple file system security structure is adequate for most purposes. It consists of six levels:

1. **Read**. The information can be observed or read.

2. **Write**. The information can be modified.

3. **Create**. This type of information can be created.

4. **Delete**. This information can be removed.

5. **Execute**. If this information is a program or script, it can be executed.

6. **Use/Publish**. This information can be used for internal purposes and/or published and released.

Depending on the type of information that you handle and the organization you are dealing with, you may well be able to use fewer categories (Read, Write/Create/Delete, and Execute/Use/Publish, are three fairly useful categories).

As before, if you are having trouble identifying the level of security, it is probably either because the secured object is too general or because you need to list several levels of security for several classes of users.

Identify the Owner

Finally, for each secured object, you must have an owner: someone who can approve all of these changes.

Security Tips

Here are a few tips to help you set up security.

- **Include everything**. Do not adopt a policy that if it is uncategorized it is not secure. Security is not just a help in determining what cannot be released, it is a help in determining what can be released. By having security in place before you need it, not only can you prevent problems but you can avoid confusion and delays.

- **Do not make it too complicated**. Security is designed to get in the way of efficient operations. Do not make it more intrusive than necessary. If you do, people will avoid it.

- **Secured objects need not be disjoint**. The information on a Web page may be subject to different security than the page itself. If this starts to pose a problem, deal with it then. However, in most cases you can move along with no problems having such overlap. (If you have database-driven Web pages, this situation will exist since the database data is subject to different security mechanisms than the pages on which it is displayed.)

- **Keep your security updated**. People leave and join organizations.

- **Do it as you go along**. Tag each Web page you produce with a security level. That is easier than reviewing an entire Web site (which can take months).

- **Whatever you do, do it**. Using the Internet means people have access to your data; in addition, the Web-based enterprise frequently uses more consultants and part-timers than traditional organizations. You cannot imagine what information may be of interest to people (in addition to the obviously interesting information—which may actually not matter).

Privacy

In the previous section, the emphasis was on the security of data that you own or control. Privacy deals quite often with safeguarding information that you do not own and over which your control is temporary.

For example, the office telephone number of your employees is your information to release or not as you see fit. The home telephone numbers of your employees may or may not be information that you can release. Just as Web caches may contain data that needs to be secured, so, too, many components of the Internet may contain data that is collected in the normal course of operations and which should not be passed on. (This is really no different from a hotel telephone operator who is asked to place a call to a movie star: the operator may find it interesting to have the star's home phone number, but it must not be passed on.)

You are involved in privacy because a remarkably large amount of information that is similar to the movie star's phone number comes your way when you run a Web site or network. You have implicit and explicit responsibilities with regard to the data that you collect or otherwise obtain.

Note that these responsibilities vary from place to place. The European Union's policies on Web privacy are somewhat stricter than those in other places, such as the United States. Consult a legal advisor to know what your responsibilities are.

You use the techniques of security in order to keep private information private. Here are the steps that you need to take to implement a privacy policy.

Have a Privacy Policy

You must have a privacy policy. In many places, this is required by law (although many Web sites do not do so). TRUSTe, sponsored by AOL, Compaq, Ernst & Young LLP, Excite, Intel, Microsoft, and Novell, can help you develop a customized privacy statement for your Web site using their step-by-step wizard on their Web site (www.truste.org).

Internal Web sites may not need privacy policies: your organization's personnel policies may be sufficient. However, unless you are certain that everyone using your site will be very clear when they are on your site and when they are on other Internet sites, you may need to repeat the policy on your site.

Be Careful What Data You Collect	You do not have to protect the privacy of information you do not collect. If you use questionnaires, forms, or other feedback devices on your site, examine the cost of storing and protecting the information you are asking for.
Allow the Policy to Change	Provide a means for updating the policy and notifying people of those changes. You may not be engaged in e-commerce now, but you may do so in the future. You may not plan a periodic electronic newsletter now, but it, too, may happen in the future. Your policies with regard to handling e-mail addresses and other information need to be able to be modified over time.

Summary

You can control where people use your Web site: where they are located, where the servers are located, and where your organization is located. You also have total control over the virtual place that your site has—whether it is designed for children or for adults, whether it is public or open only to paying customers, and so forth. Too often, people simply fall into arrangements that may or may not be necessary. In designing your Web presence, decide how you want to control these locations.

Security and privacy are often ignored until their absence makes headlines (and they do make good headlines). You have policies for security and privacy whether you think you do or not: you may have opted to use someone else's policies, and they may not be appropriate.

In all of these cases, the important point is to deal with these issues before they become crises. They are part of setting up and managing the Web-based enterprise.

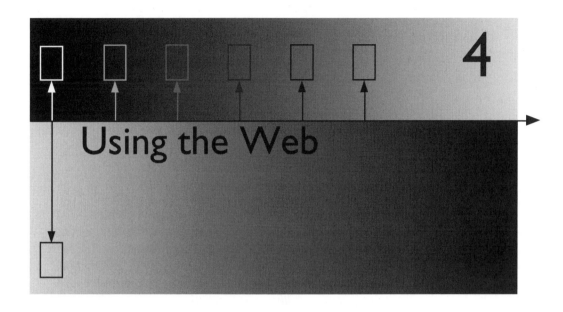

Using the Web

4

In the first chapter of this book, you have seen what a Web-based enterprise is, how it can evolve, and where within (or outside) an organization it can spring from. Then, in Chapter 2, the issues involved in individual interaction with the Web were explored. The previous chapter examined the places (real and virtual) involved in using the Web along with security and privacy issues.

These are all background material for you to think about as you plan your next step: actually using the Web. This chapter helps you pull it all together and get on your way; it addresses the issues involved in getting started and managing a Web-based enterprise.

The chapter addresses a number of basic issues:

- *"What Are You Doing on the Web?" This section helps you set your objectives.*

- *"Who Are You Doing It For?" Scores of millions of people have access to the Web, but who among them are you dealing with?*

- *"What Resources Do You Have?" Rather than start your project with a protracted corporate battle, why not look at what you have to work with and begin there?*

- *"What Do You Control?" In the real world, not everything is under your control. These are some of the areas to worry about.*

- *But first... "Ethics" is a review of some of the concerns that have been expressed in previous chapters and in other venues. This is a reality check: you need to make certain that what you plan to do is achievable, worth doing, and that you intend to do it in an appropriate manner. Remember that the Web is a very public world, and the eyes of friends, neighbors, colleagues, and competitors are strong enforcers of communal norms. (In other words, make sure you mean it if you send out 4 million spam e-mails.)*

- *"Planning to Use the Web" is the step-by-step guide to actually getting started.*

This chapter ends the first part of the book; in the next part, you will look at specific aspects of pages and sites in some detail. It is no accident that this chapter precedes the more technical chapters. Make your choices about how you will use the Web before the technology intrudes. Do your research by surfing the Web and examining what you want to do in your enterprise. By the time you have bought your database, set up your Web server, and flipped the coin to choose JavaScript or Visual Basic, you will be too deeply immersed in the trees to see the forest.

What Are You Doing on the Web?

First, you need to answer the most basic question of all: what are you doing on the Web? From the individual activities described in Chapter 2 and the types of places described in Chapter 3, what is it that you want people to do, and what type of place do you want to create?

It is usually far easier to answer what you want to do or what you want people to do; it is also easier to answer the type of place you want to create. Think, for a while, about your clients, customers, and users.

Although sections of your site may have varying purposes, your overall site purpose is likely to be one of the following choices. (If your site serves several classes of users—such as customers, internal staff, media, shareholders, and researchers—you need to choose one of these options for each class of user, as described in the next section.)

Here are the choices for the purpose of a site:

- **Duplication**. Provide the information and services that you provide in non-Web ways.

- **Expansion**. Provide additional information and services on the Web that you do not provide elsewhere.

- **Substitution**. Provide a different set of information and services than you provide in non-Web ways.

- **Replacement**. Replace non-Web information and services with the Web.

Duplicating Non-Web Services

In this case, you need to ascertain first just what you provide, since you are committing to duplicate everything on the Web. This is sometimes easier said than done. For a company with a variety of locations (a bank, a store, a consultancy, and so forth), opening a duplicative Web site is just like opening a new branch location.

In other cases, duplicating non-Web services is merely a matter of providing online entry of data. A newspaper can duplicate its classified ad department on the Web by providing a simple form to be filled out.

Expanding on Non-Web Services

Expansion starts from duplication and then adds to it. In other words, you create a Web branch or location and then provide information and/or services there that you do not provide in a typical branch or location.

Some of these additional services are a matter of the Web's very nature (such as 24-hour availability or access from any Web-connected device in the world); others (such as special ordering or carrying items with low turnover) may be economical only in a Web-based environment.

In the world of information, the equivalent of low-turnover stock can be very small transactions. As a consultant, you may not be able to undertake a half hour or one hour project: the overhead of preparing a proposal, setting up a meeting, and so forth is not worth it. On the Web, this type of expansion may be feasible.

In short, expansion normally consists of:

- Doing more of what you normally do (at off-hours, in faraway places)

- Doing things you normally cannot do

Newspapers and television news bureaus frequently provide material on their Web sites that goes beyond what they publish on paper. This type of expansion falls into both categories: it is more of the same activity, and it is something that they normally cannot do (due to the constraints of paper, length of broadcasts, and so forth).

Substituting for Non-Web Services

If you are a cosmetologist, you will find it rather difficult to squeeze that lipstick over an Internet connection. However, you may have a thriving business providing online advice—either individually or through generic advice on your Web site. You will find a multitude of such businesses on the Web.

Replacing Non-Web Services

Finally, you may be using the Web to replace real-world activities. You may provide online entry of data as a duplicate of paper-based entry, but you may also decide to replace paper-based entry with Web-based data entry.

This happened in the mid-1990s in many areas of employment. By accepting only online applications, recruiters were able to access a larger pool of applicants than they otherwise would have seen; they also automatically screened out people without computer skills.

Who Are You Doing It For?

One of these options is appropriate for each major class of user: typically, you will select one of these options for your internal operational staff and one for your users, customers, or clients. Decide whom you are addressing with your site and what option is right for each.

Do not worry about having a wide variety of types of users: one is often sufficient, and that is your clientele. In describing your users, make certain to exclude users where appropriate. If you do not care about sightseers, or if your site is appropriate only for veterinarians (rather than pet owners), make that clear—to yourself, and on the site.

What Resources Do You Have?

At this point—before you have decided what the site looks like or what it should contain—inventory your resources. Is it you on a weekend once a month? Can you get a staff together? Are they full-time or part-timers?

When it comes to your computer resources, do you have an existing hypertext transfer protocol (HTTP) or Web server to use? Does your organization have an Internet service provider (ISP)? Will you use your own technology resources?

In most existing enterprises, you do not have the luxury of starting from scratch. In these cases, the site is built around the people and resources that you have. The alternative is to prepare a project plan and go out and fight for the resources you need: in the fast-paced world of the Internet, it is almost always better to do what you can now.

What Do You Control?

Also at the start, take a cold-eyed view at what you control. Work with it if at all possible; again, the alternative is spending your time on internal struggles, not getting the site up.

Site Design and Maintenance

If you are part of a larger organization, your particular Web site may have to be part of the larger whole. Know this before you start.

Operations	Will you run your Web site? Will an ISP run it? An internal technology department? Many, many corporate Web sites have become hot potatoes, tossed from one group to another. When things are going well, everyone wants credit; when the site crashes, no one takes the blame. Establish operational control in advance of both good times and bad.
Content	Can you put up your own Web site or are there corporate legal and other constraints and reviews? Since the Web is a new adventure for many organizations, you—and they—may not be aware of these constraints. If you are a member of a professional or trade group, it may have a say about your site's content.
Chats and User Updates	If you are going to allow updates to your site—including chats—by users, they have a degree of control. Will you preview such user input? Take no responsibility? In many cases, a middle ground is the shakiest legal position. The solution can be achieved in either of two ways: understand your legal position or do not allow chats and user updates.
International Constraints	The Web is a borderless medium. Nevertheless, countries have a variety of evolving laws that deal with it. Everything from financial services to pornography and gambling is subject to varying laws.

Practical Constraints	Face reality: do you want the best site in the world or the best site that can be created by such and such a date? Do you want to spend all of your efforts on getting the site up, or do you want to save resources for its maintenance?
Personnel Constraints	Yes, it is possible that you or your staff will become highly adept at building and maintaining a site, but is that realistic? Is that something you want to do?

Ethics

The Web is a new field and one that evolves rapidly. There are tremendous opportunities and excitement. Make certain that you have constant reality checks. Are you (or your staff) working 80 hours a week? Is your enthusiasm encouraging you to cut corners on testing?

What about your relations with outside vendors and consultants? Are you taking advantage of them? Or they of you?

This is a topic that is all too often ignored; however, it is amazing how quickly tempers can fray in a high-pressure environment. In practical terms, ethics matter tremendously in Web projects—if only because by definition the people who may become aggrieved have at their disposal an extraordinarily powerful tool to tell their side of the story (the Web).

Planning to Use the Web

It is time to get to work planning for your Web-based enterprise. The choices that you make now will have ramifications for years to come. Do not be frightened: just do not evade the choices.

The overall steps can be simply stated:

- Establishing a vocabulary
- Deciding what needs to be done
- Deciding who will do it

Talking about the Web

If you are going to use the Web, you need to talk about it. The simple statement, "Let's put up a Web site" has multiple meanings to people. Start by making certain that everyone understands the terminology and the purpose. (The previous chapters provide a theoretical basis for the Web and should be helpful in this regard.)

Creating a Vocabulary

You will be creating a new vocabulary for your organization. You will need to refer to your Web site, your Internet service provider, and possibly a variety of hardware. You will also be creating Web pages that will convey your ideas to the world.

As you come across ideas or concepts, name them. Keep a list. "Web Store" and "Online Sales" may mean the same thing to you, but if you use the terms interchangeably, people may get confused (and your site may look sloppy). Remember that people who are using your site are usually alone: there is no one to guide them.

While you are at it, start creating a style sheet for your site. Even the most graphically oriented site has plenty of text. Do you say "We welcome you…" or "PSM welcomes you…"? Is it "Web Store," "Web store," or "Location/Web"?

Comparative Web Site Studies

As you are beginning to build (or revamp) your site, spend time—a lot of time—examining other sites. Look particularly at sites that are comparable to yours (such as those of competitors); look, too, at sites that are similar to your goals but are outside your particular field.

For example, in the United States, many public library sites look much the same. (This is because many public libraries use one of only a handful of automated cataloging systems.) Search sites—such as Yahoo!, Excite, Lycos, and so forth—have very similar functions to library sites; however, while the library sites look much the same and the search sites look much the same, there is little cross-pollination.

Be careful in your studies to adopt ideas and public-domain information. There is a growing body of litigation regarding the inappropriate use of Web site tools. Ideas, though, cannot be protected by copyright or patent.

Deciding What Needs to Be Done

As your Web-based enterprise project grows, you need to use normal project management techniques. Know what needs to be done and by when. The biggest challenge for most Web-based enterprises is integrating Web operations into the rest of the organization. Somehow, standard planning and scheduling techniques seem to disappear.

Appendix A is a checklist for what needs to be done in your Web-based enterprise. In addition to helping you plan the project, it provides a Web site registry template that you can use to track your site and its pages. The concepts and terminology of the body of the book are reflected in the checklist and registry.

Deciding Who Will Do It

Your major choice is whether to build your Web-based enterprise with internal staff or with consultants and freelancers.

Planning for Enterprise-Wide Integration, Adoption, and Support

The temptation is to put a Web project in its own compartment of an organization. This may mean a large enterprise establishing a Web team and putting them in an office together; in a one-person organization, this may mean that you deal with the Web project on weekends.

If at all possible, integrate the project as thoroughly as possible with the organization as a whole. When it is off to the side, it tends to veer off into a technological morass; enterprise-wide goals and objectives get lost. Furthermore, you easily wind up with your business experience in one group and the technological experience in another.

The Role of Consultants and Contractors

You may not have the resources to build your own Web site. Consultants and contractors can be very useful in helping out. However, remember that maintaining a Web site is a constant operation. Hiring someone to build a Web site—and then disappear—is an invitation to disaster (and a common one, at that).

Hiring consultants and contractors to train your staff (new or existing) can be very productive. Furthermore, recognize that the site will need maintenance. In talking to consultants and contractors at the beginning of a project, focus on how the site will be maintained next year. The wonderful graphics you see may blind you to the fact that there is a lot of hard (and boring) work maintaining the site.

Planning for Maintenance

It cannot be stressed enough that putting up a Web site is only the first step—and a small one at that. The site will need to be maintained. Not only will conditions in the world and your enterprise change, but there will be changes in your technological environment and changes both to hardware and software.

You must plan for these: not doing so always ends in trouble.

Summary

The ease with which Web sites can be created sometimes encourages people to launch poorly thought-out enterprises and adventures. Plan your Web-based enterprise and its manifestation on the Web—your site—with as much care as you would devote to building a traditional facility or organizing any activity.

Start by deciding just what it is that you plan to do on the Web. Continue by identifying for whom you are doing it and what resources you have available to do it with. Set a plan and then implement it, always allowing for the changes that occur when the real world intervenes in your best-laid plans.

With this high-level planning, you can move on to the next part of the book: the actual implementation and management of the site and its pages.

II

Sites and Pages: Design and Maintenance

You see your Web-based-enterprise in its entirety: you know the people, organization, and facilities behind it. To your clients, customers, and visitors, your Web site and its pages are your enterprise. They see nothing else. (That is why creating a clearly defined sense of place is so important.)

The first part of this book dealt with behavior: how people use the Web and computers, where they use them, what their expectations are, and how you can start to build your Web-based enterprise. This part of the book is about Web pages and sites themselves. This part of the book helps you look at Web pages, identify their components, and then use the specific code necessary to create (or modify) those components.

75

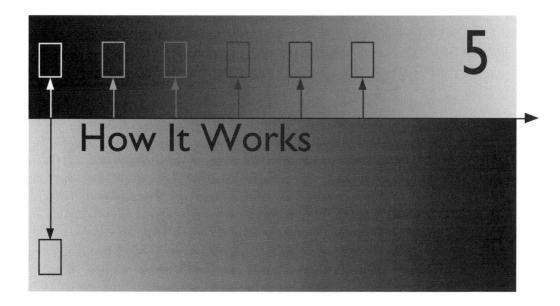

How It Works

5

The issues in this part of the book are bigger than the simple HTML formatting issues such as whether tables or frames are best to implement a certain page design. These are the high-level concerns that are frequently overlooked.

To begin with, this chapter deals with some of the background issues of the Web. It covers some Internet basics as well as critical basics for the Web-based enterprise (such as communicating with users).

The sections of this chapter are:

- *"The Nets." Not long ago it seemed clear that the Internet was a public network and that it was quite distinct from private, geographically constrained local area networks. To-*

day, the Internet coexists with intranets, virtual private networks, extranets, and other technologies. This section provides a brief overview of them.

- *"The Mechanics of the Web." Here the three protocols you need to deal with are described. They are HTTP, HTML, and FTP. HTTP is used to request and deliver Web pages, HTML is used to code Web pages, and FTP is used to upload Web pages from the computer where they are edited to the server.*

- *"Communicating with Users." This part of the chapter shows you how to implement e-mail and forms for feedback; it also covers how to dynamically create pages—often in response to a user request—and it describes how the Web page author can run software on the user's computer.*

- *"The Next Generation: XHTML and Cascading Style Sheets." These new technologies are starting to appear; here is information on how to prepare for them.*

The Nets

You will hear much talk of intranets, extranets, virtual private networks, tunneling, and other arcane terms. This section is a very brief and high-level overview of some of the technologies that may matter to you.

How the Internet Works

The Internet is a packet-switched network. What that means is that all messages are broken into small pieces (**packets**); each packet is addressed separately to the computer that should receive it. The address information contains additional information that allows the receiving computer to reconstruct the message from the various packets that are received.

Packets that are received by computers to which they are not addressed are simply routed onward to the next computer on the Internet, which will (presumably) either process the message or route it on again until it reaches its destination. This method of communication does not require an end-to-end link as is the case in a telephone conversation. The packets do eventually end up traveling an end-to-end link, but it generally is not created all at one time. Furthermore, this method of transmitting messages means that if there is a problem on the network, packets can be rerouted around it.

Tunneling

In order to optimize communications, you can interfere with this basic structure as long as it appears to be preserved. For example, some organizations have optimized routing tables that designate more complete paths for the packets to traverse (in other words, instead of the packet being shot off in the general direction of Los Angeles, it is hand-carried to the corner of Hollywood and Vine). **Tunneling** is one such technique.

Intranets

A private network can be established that uses Internet technology but is not connected to the public Internet. Such a network is an **intranet**; its nodes are private because there is no physical connection to the Internet.

An intranet can use all of the Internet's protocols (and software) for the Web, e-mail, and so forth. Since there is no connection to the Internet, only the Web sites and e-mail addresses on the intranet are available.

For many organizations, an intranet is not physically separated from the Internet. Its separation is accomplished with a **firewall**—a computer that monitors traffic into and out of the intranet. The traffic can be limited by message types, by physical terminal identifiers, specific sites, and so forth.

Most organizations that connect any type of internal network to the Internet have some form of firewall. In addition, some individuals have some type of firewall installed to provide security for their files.

Firewalls are particularly important for networks and individual computers that are connected to the Internet at all times and that have a static IP address. This includes networks and individual computers connected to the Internet using cable, DSL, and ISDN connections. Dial-up connections are transient and normally do not have static IP addresses—a new address is generated with each connection. The importance of the static IP address is that someone can attempt over a period of time to connect to your computer. If you are running a Web site, this is a good thing. If you are balancing your checkbook and believe that your hard disk is not visible to hackers, having a static IP address and no firewall may be a snare and a delusion.

Extranets

An intranet's firewall can also allow access to the intranet to users with appropriate IDs and passwords. When an intranet is accessible in this way, it is referred to as an **extranet**.

Virtual Private Networks

Connections can be set up among intranets and other types of local area networks (that is, local area networks using protocols other than Internet protocols). These connections can be physical such as leased telecommunications lines. However, they can also be virtual. In the latter case, the resultant network is referred to as a **virtual private network**.

In a virtual private network, the connection between the networks is usually made secure not only by encryption but also by limiting it to specific, known, Internet addresses. Frequently, tunneling is used to speed the connections and to guarantee them.

Caches

Finally, you should be aware of an issue that is increasingly important on the Internet: caching. Your Web browser has a cache in which it stores recently visited pages. You may not realize that your Internet service provider probably also has a cache in which recently visited pages for all of the customers are stored. An Internet service provider can make its service perkier by efficiently caching frequently accessed pages.

Likewise, an organization can distribute mirror copies of its frequently accessed pages to Internet service providers and other locations on the net. This makes that organization's site performance better.

Because of the potential significant improvements in performance, a great deal of work on caching is now going on.

Why This Matters

As you develop your site, be aware of caches. You can work within the system by carefully using expiration dates on your Web pages, allowing them to be cached. (Estimates are that a shockingly low number of Web pages are cached—mostly because their authors inadvertently prevent them from being so.)

Note, too, that out-of-date copies of your Web pages may proliferate if you do not do this properly.

What You Can Do

With regard to these terms—tunneling, intranets, extranets, virtual private networks, and caches—it is important to understand what they are. It is also important to remember that before you decide you need one of these technologies, make certain that you understand what you intend to accomplish with it. The extranet salesperson is in the business of selling extranets: your goal may be to improve communications within your organization, and the extranet is not necessarily the best choice. In the worst case, these are buzzwords that wind up costing you a lot of money, wasting a lot of time, and not dealing with the issues that matter to you.

The Mechanics of the Web

There are two protocols involved in viewing Web pages: hypertext transfer protocol (HTTP) and hypertext markup language (HTML). HTTP is used to request and deliver a resource (Web page); HTML is used to format the Web page's content. File transfer protocol (FTP) is used behind the scenes to maintain your site. They are discussed in this section.

In addition, caching is covered here. It interacts with the HTTP and HTML protocols, and it affects how pages are disseminated across the Web.

HTTP

When you type a uniform resource locator (URL) into your Web browser, you are requesting that an Internet resource be delivered to you using the HTTP protocol. The transmission is between an HTTP server at the remote site and your browser. In many cases, the HTTP server simply retrieves a file from its disk and sends it your way; it knows nothing about the Web, and it is only when your browser encounters the file that it takes shape as a Web page.

In other cases, the HTTP server asks a separate Web server to create a Web page and prepare it to be transmitted to you. Logically, these are two separate operations: transmission (HTTP) and Web page formatting (HTML). However, many products combine the two, and as a result you will find HTTP server used interchangeably with Web server in many places. They are different.

There are four parts to a URL:

1. The first part (the **scheme**) is the protocol to be used. It is followed by a colon. http: is the scheme for Web pages.

2. The second part is the **host**—the entity to which the request is made. A host must uniquely identify something on the network; if its name is not unique, requests could be routed to one entity at one time and to another one at other times. Hosts are introduced by two slashes—//.

3. The third part is the **path**—the fully qualified name of the Web page in most cases. (Fully qualified means that the name includes all of the directories or folders in which it is located. The names of the directories are separated by slashes—/.)

4. The fourth part is the **searchpart**—optional parameters that allow you to pass data to databases, programs, and scripts on the host. It is introduced by a question mark (?).

On some operating systems, capitalization matters—Index.html is not the same file as index.html. On other operating systems, capitalization does not matter. It is the operating system of the host—your HTTP server—that determines this. Since you do not always know if your HTTP server is case sensitive, it is best to pretend that it is and to be careful always to use the standard capitalization (however you define it).

Hosts

The host part of a URL uniquely identifies a resource on the network in one of two ways: it can use an IP address—a set of four numbers separated by dots—or it can use a name that includes a domain name such as www.philmontmill.com. Domain names are assigned by Internet registration agencies, and they constitute a link to IP addresses.

Your ISP can identify an agency for you, or they can take care of the registration. The entire process is now under the aegis of the Internet Corporation for Assigned Names and Numbers (ICANN). The major provider of registration services for the .com, .net, and .org domains has been Network Solutions (www.networksolutions.com); however, many more registrars now exist. The registration process involves linking the domain name to the IP address; therefore, you must already have your ISP selected and you must have an IP address. You can change the address if you move ISPs. (Some registrars allow registration without an IP address to reserve a domain name.)

Creating or changing the address for a domain name requires some time—often a day—for the change to be propagated throughout Internet routers. As a result, it is often best to do this at the start of a weekend or other slow time. Observe how your registration agency processes updates, and you will be able to see when to time your update.

Domain names vary from country to country; in the United States, they often end in .com, .gov, .edu, .mil, or .org. In other countries, they often end in a pair of codes such as .co.uk or .co.fr (commercial sites in the United Kingdom or France). The single word before the suffix is added to the suffix to create the domain name—as in yourcompany.com or yourcompany.co.fr.

The word (or words) preceding the domain name (often "www") is the name of a computer at the site. A large site may have many servers—www.sales.bigcompany.com can handle Web traffic, mail.bigcompany.com can handle mail, and so forth.

You can use either the domain name–based URL or an IP address–based URL—

```
http://www.philmontmill.com/index.html
http://123.456.789.123/index.html
```

However, in almost all cases it is preferable to use the domain name–based URL. If you move your site from one computer to another, you need to update the global Internet registration tables and then all traffic is rerouted accordingly. If you use an

IP address–based URL, you need to notify everyone of the new address. (This conversion of domain names to IP addresses is accomplished by the domain name system—DNS—and domain name servers, which are located throughout the Internet.)

The host name (either domain name based or IP address based) uniquely identifies a computer. However, sometimes a single computer needs to be able to function as if it were two or more computers—for example, it may be running two HTTP servers. This is accomplished by breaking down each host using port numbers. An HTTP server is said to listen to a specific port: traffic that is directed to that computer is directed via port number to one HTTP server or another. The port number is always used, but if it has a default value (80 for HTTP) it can be omitted from the URL. If used, however, it follows the host and is separated from it by a colon (:) as in

```
http://www.philmontmill.com:591/index.html
http://123.456.789.123:591/index.html
```

Paths

Following the host name and optional port, a slash introduces the path or name of the resource being requested. When a Web site is set up, a directory is established on the HTTP server; all of the files for the site are located in that directory. (In the previous example, the file being requested is index.html.)

As a site grows, it makes sense to use folders or directories to organize it. Thus, within your Web site's directory, you might create a subdirectory (or folder) called "employees." A request for a file in that subdirectory called "policies.html" would look like this:

```
http://www.yourdomain.com/employees/policies.html
```

Most HTTP servers have default files that they serve up if no path name is provided. These files typically are named default.htm or index.html. Someone who types in

```
http://www.yourdomain.com
```

will automatically get such a file (if it exists).

Note that the naming of these default files is set up for the HTTP server: you will be told what the default name is.

Typically, the files on your Web site will end with .htm or .html. Again, this is a characteristic of the HTTP server; you will be told how to name your files. (Other suffixes are used for graphics files.)

Searchparts

Searchparts provide parameters and data to be passed to the HTTP server. They are discussed in *Database-Driven Web Sites*.

Who Does What with HTTP

Putting together your site involves a number of steps taken by a number of different parties. Table 5-1 shows the steps involved and who is responsible for them. The steps are roughly in the sequence in which you will need to carry them out.

Note that your ISP may fulfill two roles that are separated in the table. Your ISP always provides connectivity—the link from your HTTP server to the Internet. Your ISP may also actually operate your HTTP server (this is often called Web hosting); however, in other cases, your HTTP server will be under your control and at your location. In such cases the ISP provides connectivity and you maintain the HTTP server.

Step	Who Is Responsible
The IP address of your Web site	Your ISP
Your domain name (such as philmontmill.com)	Registration agency

TABLE 5-1. Setting Up a Web Site

Step	Who Is Responsible
The name of your HTTP server (in www.philmontmill.com it is www)	HTTP server operator
The directory on the HTTP server in which your Web pages are stored	HTTP server operator
Suffixes for Web pages (usually .htm or .html)	HTTP server operator
Port number (if needed)	HTTP server operator
Folders or subdirectories within that directory	You
Names of Web pages	You
Creating html files	You
Moving html files to your Web site	You (see "FTP" starting on page 94)

TABLE 5-1. Setting Up a Web Site (Continued)

Responding to an HTTP Request

When an HTTP server responds to a request, it actually sends a message back to the requester that has two sections: a header, with status information, and the message itself (the Web page).

HTTP Headers   The header contains at a minimum the information that a browser will need to display the page that follows. For Web pages, this minimal header consists of the following line:

```
Content-type: text/html
```

This line is generated by the HTTP server before it sends the contents of the Web page in the message body.

Other information can be sent in the HTTP header. This information is processed by the receiving HTTP client. When you are running a browser, it functions both as HTTP client and as HTML renderer (that is, the software that images the Web page). There are other HTTP clients wandering around, however, and they, too, will see the HTTP headers while not looking into the HTML.

Caching

Cache information is provided as part of the HTTP header; it will be seen by proxy servers, firewalls, and other intermediaries. This means that you can control caching at a very high level.

Caches have two primary purposes:

1. They make Web sites "perkier"—they load faster for users if parts or all of them are cached either on the user's computer or close by (for example, at the local ISP). The chief beneficiaries of this improved performance are the user, who does not have to wait for a site to load, and the site owner, who may view it as a competitive advantage. Some site owners store cached copies of their sites at strategic places around the Internet to improve their performance in this way.

2. They make the Web as a whole run faster. Less data moves, and it moves for shorter distances. All Web users benefit from this decrease in traffic, but ISPs in particular benefit because a significant part of their investment is in communications, and reducing the demand can translate directly into reduced costs.

On the other hand, caches can cause problems. Chief among these problems is the presentation of out-of-date information from a cache. For many e-business marketers, another problem is the fact that when a Web page is provided from a cache, counters on the Web page at the original server may not be updated.

The "solution" to these problems for many Web authors is to prevent their pages being cached. When coupled with the widespread lack of knowledge about caching, this means that the Web as a whole is running remarkably inefficiently simply because caching is not used appropriately. Before you buy your way out of performance problems with added hardware and communications lines, consider whether you are using caching appropriately. [1]

The HTTP header can contain two pieces of caching information. This information applies to the entire HTTP message; it is read and processed by any entity that is processing the HTTP message. Thus, routers and other network computers can see it. (They do not examine the content of the message.)

Expires   The Expires header contains an Internet date and time. This is expressed in Universal (Greenwich mean) time, and it has a format such as

```
Tue, 10 Jan 2000 00:00:00 GMT
```

Last-Modified   This header contains the date and the time at which the contents were last modified. It can be used by a browser or proxy server that has a cached copy. An HTTP request can be used to validate that the cached copy's last-modified value is equal to that on the HTTP server.

Cache-Control   This header was implemented in HTTP 1.1. As a result, if your HTTP server remains at version 1.0, you cannot implement it. Likewise, routers and other devices that are not yet supporting version 1.1 cannot handle it. You can control caching to a great extent with these values. For details, consult the HTTP RFC. [2]

How to Do It   Caching with HTTP headers requires those headers to be set on the HTTP server. There are several ways

---

1. The best place to start if you are looking for caching information is http://www.w3.org/Propagation/. It is the World Wide Web Consortium's page titled "Propagation, Caching and Replication on the Web."
2. You can find RFC 2616 on the Web at many locations including http://www.ietf.org/rfc/rfc2616.txt.

of doing this. One is to configure the HTTP server to insert specific caching values to files that are downloaded from various directories. Another way is to specify that certain types of files (images, for example) have certain caching characteristics. You set this up once with the manager of your HTTP server, and then you distribute your HTML files accordingly.

Another way of doing this is to insert the HTTP headers dynamically in pages that you generate using Perl, ASP, CGI, or other dynamic page generation tools. [3]

You may have to work a bit to get caching implemented on your site. Not all ISPs are equipped to help you set up the HTTP server to configure the headers. (It can be done, they just may not have the support staff.) Keep at it: the benefits are almost always worth it. And once you have set it up in one way or another, you can reuse that implementation for a variety of pages.

How to Prevent Cache Problems If you are using caching and you discover that a page needs to be changed, what do you do? Basically, the answer to this is the same as the answer to the question about how to deal with a crashed disk: by the time you ask the question, it is too late.

Caching is based on the name of the resource—the name of the HTML page, in most cases. Once you have set caching parameters for that page, that is it (unless you use the validation option no-cache). In other words, if you have said that the page is valid for a month, you can assume that it will be out there in various caches on the Internet for that month.

Of course, something may happen during that period to make the page invalid. Company names change, people quit (or die), and new products are announced. The safest way to handle this situation is to make pages noncacheable and all in-

3. For more details, see *Perl 5 Programmer's Notebook* by Jesse Feiler.

cluded images and other files cacheable. If your home page is index.html, make it noncacheable so that people get the most recent version. If your logo is used on the page, make it cacheable—you can call it logo.gif. If the logo changes, change the home page—index.html—to refer to newlogo.gif, and make that logo cacheable, too. (Do not worry about the cached copies of the old logo—caches can purge themselves in a variety of ways that are none of your business.)

HTML

HTTP is used to request and receive Web pages. The pages themselves consist of HTML—a version of standard generalized markup language (SGML) which itself is an outgrowth of IBM's Generalized Markup Language (GML). It is discussed in Chapter 11 of *Database-Driven Web Sites*.

Note that HTML is now at version 4; it is just about at the point where its complexity is starting to outweigh its simple power. But do not lose sleep over this. A new technology—extensible markup language (XML)—has been devised that addresses these problems. Thus, HTML 4 is reformulated as XHTML 1. However, you should be aware that part of XHTML 1 is a tightening of rules. Some of these are noted in this section. Since well-formed HTML documents are automatically XHTML documents, you should not worry too much about this—except to make certain that your documents are well-formed. See "XHTML" starting on page 115 for more details.

HTML is a text-based language. It uses only the text characters on your keyboard. All formatting is accomplished by text commands.

HTML documents consist of elements which in turn consist of text surrounded by starting and ending tags. Tags are enclosed in < and >. Thus, the element consisting of the word "hello" in italics looks like this:

```
<i>
Hello
</i>
```

Ending tags are identical to starting tags except that they start with a /. Basic formatting tags are fairly simple to identify—i for italics, b for bold, and so forth. HTML is not case sensitive—<I> and <i> are the same tag. However, this is not true in XHTML. All HTML elements that will be used in XHTML should be in lowercase.

Elements can be embedded within other elements. Their content and/or their ending tags may be omitted if the meaning is unambiguous. (Endings tags are required in XHTML.) For example, the break element consists only of a starting tag—
—which inserts a line break. (In XHTML, you must either use an ending tag or you must place a / after the starting tag—
.)

When you look at a page of HTML, the first thing to do is to line up starting and ending tags so that you can identify the elements on the page. If you are using an HTML editor, often this formatting will be done automatically for you. If you are using a visual editor, you can switch between the visual display and the HTML version.

HTML Elements

The preceding points are illustrated by the HTML element itself. The entire Web page consists of a single element. Within it are other elements that contain its content.

Thus, an empty HTML page consists only of the starting and ending tags as shown here:

```
<html>
</html>
```

HTML Head

Within the html element is a single HTML HEAD element. Together, they look like this:

```
<html>
<head>
</head>
</html>
```

The head element may contain a variety of elements that refer to the entire page; these include the background color or image, the title, comments, scripts used on the page, and caching information. You can omit the HEAD element, but that is bad form. Every page should at least have a title for the browser to display at the top of the user's window.

HTML Body

Following the HEAD element, the BODY element contains the other elements for the page. Putting together these elements, here is the HTML for a page titled "Sample Page" containing the italicized word, "Hello."

```
<html>
<head>
<title>Sample Page</title>
</head>
<body>
<i>
Hello
</i>
</body>
</html>
```

Note that the text—Hello—is not set off by quotes or other delimiters; it is the formatting tags that are delimited by < and >. Everything else is assumed to be presented as is. Note also that spaces do not matter in most cases. The title element, for example, uses one line; it could use three, as the italic element surrounding "Hello" does.

HTML Graphic Considerations

As Web pages have gotten more and more complex, HTML has also gotten more complex. Some people think that it may have exceeded its design tolerances; Cascading Style Sheets and XML are two ways in which the complexity of modern Web pages is tamed.

Making Fonts Look Right   One of the most troublesome aspects of Web pages is making them look the way you want them to. The original notion of HTML was that specific fonts would not be used to render Web pages. You can still see this concept in your Web browser where you are allowed to select fonts and font sizes for different types of text that is displayed on Web pages. The Web page designer is supposed to specify only that particular text should be rendered in normal, larger than normal, or smaller than normal size.

You now can specify specific fonts in your HTML page. The user's browser will attempt to use those fonts—if they are present on that computer. If not, you can specify alternative fonts. This means that you can control exactly what the page looks like as long as you can know what fonts are installed. In a corporate intranet where enterprise-wide fonts are used for documents, this is no problem. On the untamed Internet, it can be a problem.

Ultimately, you will have to choose between having a known environment on the users' machines and having Web pages that do not always look the way you think they should. Designing for this nondeterministic world can be a challenge.

Using Graphics for Formatted Text   One way of making things look the way you want them to is not to use text. You can use a graphic that incorporates text (such as a company logo), and you can display it as a graphic. In that way, the appearance will be what you expect.

Unfortunately, this does not solve all formatting problems, since the graphic is a separate file and must reside on the HTTP server to be available for downloading. If you are creating dynamic Web pages, or if the amount of text to be displayed is lengthy, using graphics can be very annoying. (If you have encountered a site where the text does not reflow when you resize the window, you are seeing text presented as a graphic.)

FTP

The Web page you view in your browser is normally a text file that resides on the HTTP server. You request it by typing in a

URL and having your browser send an HTTP request for the page to the server.

But how does it get there? What is the reverse mechanism?

You create HTML pages on your computer using an editing program. Since HTML is basically a text-based language, you can use almost any program that can create a text file. Today, though, there are many programs such as FrontPage, Home Page, DreamWeaver, and PageMill that you can use to create HTML pages with a graphical user interface. (You can switch back and forth between the graphical version and the raw HTML version.)

When the file has been created, you upload it using file transfer protocol (FTP). When your Web site is set up, the manager of the HTTP server will give you your FTP information. This will consist of the following:

- Your FTP logon ID—this may or may not be the same as your other IDs.

- Your FTP password.

- Your FTP directory. A directory on the HTTP server will contain all of your Web pages. Normally you do not even need to know what this directory is: when you log in with your FTP ID and password, you will automatically be connected to this directory. You can create subdirectories and folders within this directory. In addition, certain standard subdirectories and folders may exist at your HTTP server's discretion.

In order to upload your files to the HTTP server, you will need FTP software. This is included in many HTML editing programs; you also can use stand-alone products such as Archie, Anarchie, or Fetch. In addition, some operating systems let you log on to the FTP server just as you would log on to a remote disk; you can then drag files to your Web folder.

You can also use FTP to move files from the HTTP server back to your hard disk. You log on to the FTP directory and then reverse the process.

By definition, the HTTP server's files are your Web site. You may want to keep an entire copy of the site on one computer that you control. This is a good backup; however, most ISPs perform regular backups complete with off-site storage. (This is part of their service.)

Communicating with Users

The interactivity of basic Web pages is limited to hypertext links: you click on them and immediately are transported to another page (or another location on the same page). However, there is more interactivity on the Web.

The interactivity and dynamism of the Web lie in three general areas. They are demonstrated when you use an Internet search engine.

1. **Sending Information to a Server.** In addition to being able to request a specific page from an HTTP server, you can send information to a server in a variety of ways. On a search engine page, you type in the word or phrase for which you want to search and then click the Search button.

2. **Creating Web Pages Dynamically.** HTML pages can be constructed automatically in response to requests from users to HTTP servers. This is what happens when the search is completed. The HTML that is generated is yours alone: no one else sees that particular page unless they type in exactly the same search page

and the search engine database is not updated with new references.

3. **Interacting with the User's Computer.** Many people browse the Internet from personal computers—devices that can do a lot more than just display Web pages. Extensions to HTML allow Web pages to initiate processing on the local computer; this may enhance the interface or actually cause programs to be executed.

Sending Information to a Server

People need to be able to send information to a Web site for many reasons—ordering a product or service, providing feedback, or asking questions. There are several ways in which you can implement this.

- **E-mail.** You can place a mailto link on your page. When a user clicks on the link, the browser's e-mail window will open with a preaddressed message for the user to complete and send.

- **Forms.** You can create a form with a variety of data entry fields. You encounter these frequently on the Internet; they are usually characterized by Submit and Clear or Reset buttons. (Sometimes "Submit" is changed to a more specific term such as "Search" or "Send Your Feedback.").

Adding E-Mail to Your Page

The simplest way to add e-mail to your page is to insert some text such as, "Send us your comments at feedback@oursite.com."

Slightly more complex is adding an e-mail link to your page. E-mail links are like other HTML links; however, they use the prefix mailto rather than HTTP in their URLs. If you are using a graphical HTML editor, type in the text you want to appear—Send us your comments, then select it, and insert a link by typing the URL in the following format:

```
mailto:feedback@oursite.com
```

If you are constructing the link in a text-based editor, use the following format:

```
<A HREF="mailto:feedback@oursite.com">
Send us your comments
</A>
```

Remember that line spaces do not matter in HTML, so you can put this all on one line if you want. Also note that a mailto URL does not have slashes in it.

Using E-Mail Parameters You can set the subject and other parameters of the e-mail message in the URL. You do so by adding a searchpart to the mail URL. The searchpart is introduced by a question mark (?); if it has more than one parameter, they are separated by ampersands (&).

The allowable parameters are:

- subject
- cc
- bcc
- body

Each is specified in the same format. For example, to create an e-mail message with the subject "Test," use

```
mailto:feedback@oursite.com?subject=Test
```

To add a copy to your webmaster, use

```
mailto:feedback@oursite.com?subject=Test&
    cc=webmaster@oursite.com
```

Spaces are not allowed here. If you need one, use %20 (known as an escape sequence). Spaces are not allowed in addresses (such as cc and bcc); you can get around them in the subject line by judicious choice of words or using an underscore—

Test_Message. However, in the body of the message, you usually need them.Thus, a mail link that generates a message saying, "Please send me information" looks like this:

```
mailto:feedback@oursite.com?
    body=Please%20send%20me%20information
```

Note that the user must complete any necessary information and send the e-mail message: it is not sent automatically.

Pros and Cons of E-Mail   This is the simplest way of getting information from users. It works in most cases, but if a user does not have e-mail enabled, it will be impossible to send the message. (Most browsers support e-mail either with integrated software or by allowing you to configure other programs as their e-mail software.)

Using Forms

The problem that arises is, what do you do with the incoming mail? Are you going to read each message? In most cases you want to automate a process that is triggered by the message. One way of dealing with this is to use an e-mail program's filtering mechanism to sort incoming messages. A more powerful way is to use a scripting language such as Perl to parse the incoming message. But the most powerful way is to use HTML forms.

Forms allow you to group a variety of HTML data entry fields, drop-down/pop-up menus, radio buttons, and other input controls together. They are all placed within a FORM element, and their data is sent to a server to be processed. On the server, the data can be processed by a script (perhaps written in Perl), a custom-written program (in Java or C++), or a customized application (such as a database or an application server).

Organizing and Naming the Data   The data in a form will be contained within controls. Figure 5-1 shows part of a typical form.

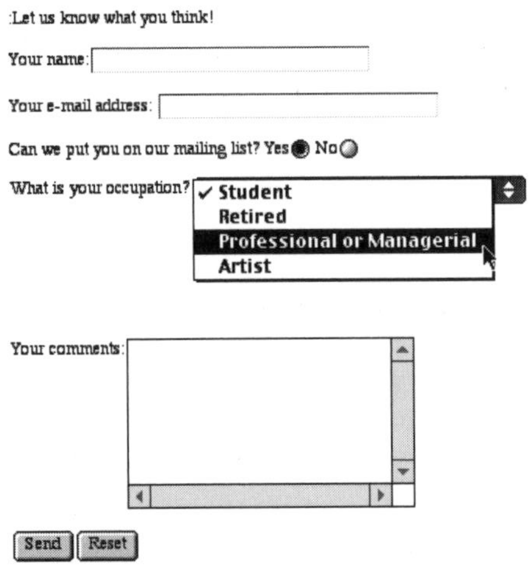

FIGURE 5-1. A Typical HTML Form

Text Fields   These are used for the entry of relatively small amounts of text. The name and e-mail fields are text fields. Here is their code:

```
<P>
Your name:<INPUT TYPE=text NAME=name VALUE="" SIZE=30>
</P>

<P>
Your e-mail address:
<INPUT TYPE=text NAME=address VALUE="" SIZE=30>
</P>
```

Each of these fields is placed in an HTML paragraph element. The label is simple text—you type it in as you wish it to appear. (The labels are underlined.) Next comes an INPUT element. Each element should be named uniquely—note the double-underlined code.

The other parameters that you can set are default values for the fields (VALUE) and the length of the fields (SIZE).

Radio Buttons The buttons for the mailing list are radio buttons. The code for them is shown here:

```
<P>
Can we put you on our mailing list?
Yes
<INPUT TYPE=radio NAME=mailinglist VALUE=oui CHECKED>
No
<INPUT TYPE=radio NAME=mailinglist VALUE=non>
</P>
```

As before, this section is also an HTML paragraph. The text— both the question and the "Yes" and "No"—is typed in. For the radio buttons, you use an INPUT element of type radio. All related radio buttons should have the same name (underlined). Within each cluster of radio buttons, each should have its own name (double-underlined code). The names need not be the same as the text labels. Furthermore, one button can have the optional CHECKED attribute.

Select A drop-down/pop-up menu is implemented with the SELECT element. The occupation entry demonstrates this. Here is the code:

```
<P>
What is your occupation?
<SELECT NAME=occupation>
      <OPTION VALUE=student>Student
      <OPTION VALUE=retired>Retired
      <OPTION VALUE=profmanag>Professional or Managerial
      <OPTION VALUE=artist>Artist
</SELECT>
</P>
```

The entire menu of choices has a name—double underlined in this example ("occupation"). For each choice, a value (underlined) is provided; this is the information that will be sent if the item is selected. Next to it, you enter the text that you want to appear. Note that in this menu, "Professional or Managerial" appears in the menu; however, the value "profmanag" is what will be sent if it is chosen.

Text Areas For text entries that are longer than one field (usually taking up more than one line), you use a text area. The Comments text area is an example. Here is the code:

```
<P>
Your comments:
<TEXTAREA NAME=comments ROWS=7 COLS=27 WRAP=virtual>
...
</TEXTAREA>
</P>
```

The form of this control is slightly different from the others. Within its paragraph, the TEXTAREA element has starting and ending tags. It may or may not have default text that is displayed. (That text is indicated by ... in the example shown.)

Each TEXTAREA must have its own name (underlined). You should set its dimensions—the number of rows displayed, the number of character positions on each row (COLS), and the WRAP parameter. WRAP determines whether text as you enter it is displayed intuitively or whether your cursor wanders off the edge of the text area. Use WRAP.

Submit and Reset Finally, the Send and Rest buttons need to be specified. Their code follows.

```
<P>
<INPUT TYPE=submit NAME=Submit VALUE="Send">
<INPUT TYPE=reset VALUE="Reset">
</P>
```

You use this code for the two buttons on any form; you may change the display on either button by using the VALUE attribute (underlined). The other values should be the same.

Putting It All Together Finally, you enclose all of these elements in a FORM element. The form element indicates to what location this data is to be sent. It is normally a URL that identifies a Perl script, an application server or database, or a custom-written program.

You can use either a POST or GET action to transmit the data. GET is used for relatively small amounts of data. It constructs a string consisting of the names of each element (such as name, e-mail, comments, and so forth), followed by the data. The string is started by a question mark (?) and each element is separated from the next by an ampersand (&). The start of such a string might be as follows:

```
?name=Sophia&email=sophia@yoursite.com&occupation=student
```

As with the mailto URL, blanks are not allowed; the user's browser will replace them with %20. You need not worry about this.

However, you do need to worry about the fact that this data is transmitted quite visibly. It is actually not the data itself that can be troubling: rather, it is the names of the data elements. If you are using a database, you may be revealing enough of its structure to let people browse fields whose names they should not know (or should be forced to guess).

On the other hand, making the variable data visible can be quite useful. The data in the searchpart is used to determine caching. If one person requests the same information twice (or if two people request the same information), cached copies can be provided (subject to caching rules discussed previously).

In the case of a POST action, the data is encoded into the body of a message. This is suitable for large amounts of data. Furthermore, it allows complex data types (graphics and video, for example) to be transmitted. And it increases security.

The FORM element consists of starting and ending tags with all intermediate form data between them. For a GET action FORM, here is what those tags might look like:

```
<FORM
    ACTION="http://www.yoursite.com/cgi-bin/formprocessor.pl"
    METHOD=POST>
...
</FORM>
```

For a POST action form, here are the corresponding tags:

```
<FORM
    ACTION="http://www.yoursite.com/cgi-bin/formprocessor.pl"
    METHOD=POST>
...
</FORM>
```

In both cases, the form data is directed to a Perl program called formprocessor.pl. It is located in a subdirectory called cgi-bin. (This is a common subdirectory for scripts and programs. Your ISP may set it up for you and you may be required to put scripts and programs there.) The suffix .pl identifies this as a Perl script on many systems.

The script or program must be prepared to accept the incoming data: it must check for the named data elements and do something with the values that are returned.

Pros and Cons of Forms   Forms are simple to implement—all HTML editors let you easily draw text fields, radio buttons, and the like. They structure the user's input and retain that structure as the data is passed on to the server.

The chief problem with forms is that something on the server needs to decode the data. Depending on your environment, you may have one or more (or none!) of the tools necessary for the job. Compounding the problem is that the tools you need to use may not correspond to your staff. Fortunately, basic processing of form data is not difficult.

The best way to decide which tool(s) to use is to examine what you want to do and to consider the end points of the transaction: the user and the database or other destination of the data. The intermediate steps are subsidiary to this overall purpose. So do not say, "This definitely needs Perl" only to find out that having parsed the data with Perl you have no place to put it. Rather, knowing where the data will go, you can easily find the missing link. If your ISP does not support the necessary link, ask if they have an alternative; if they do not, go shopping for another ISP. These tools are part of a modern ISP's services.

Creating Web Pages Dynamically

The second case in which you may need to extend basic HTML capabilities is when content needs to be presented dynamically: that is, when an HTML page needs to be created by the HTTP server on demand.

The most common way in which this is done is for a program or script on the server to run and to generate the HTTP headers and the HTML page. That program or script can go off and do anything it wants—access a database, communicate to other computers, and so forth—in order to get the information that it needs.

There are two basic ways in which this can be done:

1. When the user requests a URL, a program or script can be run. It starts when the request is received and terminates when its output (the HTTP headers and the HTML content) is returned to the HTTP server. These programs run on the HTTP server or on another computer that is connected to that server; they are written in languages such as Perl, Java, C, and C++.

2. An already-running program receives the request that is passed on from the HTTP server. It generates the output and returns it to the server. This program is running before the request is received and it continues to run afterward. Application servers and databases

are two examples of this case. In addition, the HTTP server itself can process the dynamic request in some cases. JavaServer Pages (JSP) and Active Server Pages (ASP) are created by servers in this way.

The information that is received is a standard HTTP header and a standard HTML page; your browser does not know that they have been produced on the fly. (That is why this technology works so well: the components are quite compartmentalized.)

Why You May Want to Do This

There are two reasons to use dynamically created Web pages:

1. For changing information or for variable requests, you do not have the time or resources to prepare separate HTML pages by hand. (Think of a search engine: could anyone possibly prepare the results pages for every possible search?)

2. Dynamically created Web pages can frequently be produced more easily than hand-coded pages. The design work is done once, and the data—whatever it is— is placed into the template automatically.

As you can see, both of these reasons share a common concern: dynamically created Web pages are often more efficient.

Creating a Dynamic Web Page   The Web page previously described in Chapter 3 is repeated here as Figure 5-2. It is used to demonstrate how a dynamically built Web page can reduce development time.

Two frames are used on this page (see "Composite Pages (Frames)" starting on page 137 for more details). The frame at the right is built dynamically from a database. In order to update this page, no HTML needs to be created; all that is done is to log on to the administrator's Web site and to update the data in a form. Figure 5-3 shows the data for one of the entries in Figure 5-2.

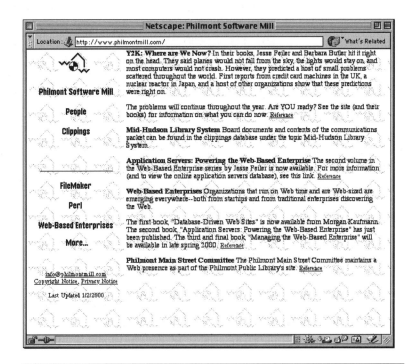

FIGURE 5-2. Philmont Software Mill Home Page

This is a standard HTML form; it uses many of the input controls described earlier in this chapter. When the Edit Record (Submit) button is clicked, the data is sent to a database from which it can be retrieved for the Web page.

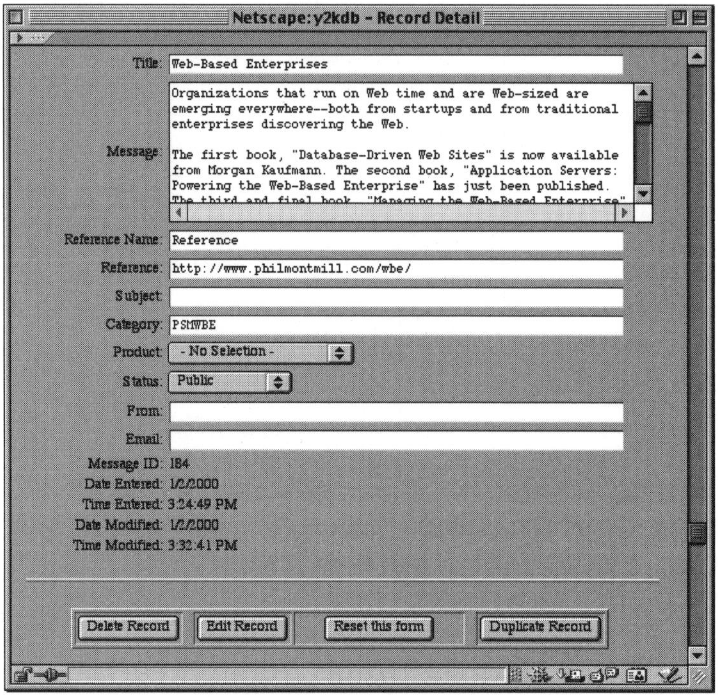

FIGURE 5-3. Input for Philmont Software Mill Home Page

The coding on the Web page is simple:

- Select all items in the database with PSM in the category. (Other codes are used to sort for other purposes.) Also, include only items with Status equal to "Public."

- For each one, place the Title field in bold.

- Follow the Title field with the contents of the Message field.

- Add the contents of the Reference Name field (this can be "Report," "URL," "White Paper," "For further information," and so forth).

- Place the URL as a link behind the Reference Name field.

Note that this process is fundamentally the same whether the criteria for selection ("PSM" in the category, for example) are chosen by the Web page designer or by the user. That is how the two uses of dynamically created Web pages merge.

This is one example of a database-driven Web page; some points should be noted:

- Although this example presents only text, most databases and dynamic Web page creation software can move images and complex media types such as video from the database to the Web page.

- Many dynamic pages present only a single record at a time—in other words, the equivalent of Title, Message, Reference Name, and Reference fields.

- This database structure is remarkably useful for a number of purposes. It organizes the information on a Web page (or part of a Web page) in the way a skilled editor would.

- The URLs can be external or internal links. If you wish to incorporate documents (text, PDF, or others), you can place them on a server by uploading them via FTP. Those links can then be placed here.

What You Need to Do This

In order to create Web pages dynamically, you need something on the HTTP server (or connected to it) that can do what you need done. Here the simplicity of the Web suddenly disintegrates before your eyes. Your choices range from simple scripting languages such as Perl to heavy-duty databases such as Oracle and IBM's DB2.

In deciding what you need, start by sketching out what you want to do (perhaps using the page shown here as an example). You will discover that almost all of the products can handle this type of process.

Here are the decision points to consider:

- What hardware and software resources do you already have? If you have an HTTP server (or have an ISP), what products are supported?

- What developmental resources do you already have? Do you have someone who knows Perl and no one who knows DB2?

- What are the costs of deploying the software? There is an enormous range. Perl, for example, is distributed free under the Perl Artistic License; Microsoft Internet Information Server is sold with a minimum number of licenses—you normally cannot buy just one to test with; and so forth.

- What are the performance characteristics? If your site gets—or is expected to get—scores of thousands of hits an hour, its needs are different from those of sites with far fewer hits. (Note that the vast majority of Internet sites do not need high performance support. For every amazon.com, there are thousands of sites for organizations such as the Philmont Public Library, Performing Arts Books, Housing Resources of Columbia County, and others.)

Pros and Cons

Creating and updating Web pages of this nature are very simple. The basic step of creating a layout need be done only once for each type of page. Those templates can be uploaded (usually via FTP) to the server or program that will merge them with the dynamic data.

Further updates—additions, deletions, and modifications to data—can be done using a form such as that shown previously. Using a form means that the information can be entered by anyone with a Web browser: HTML is not part of that picture.

A positive by-product of using dynamically created Web pages is that you are forced to consider the logical and physical design of each page as a whole. It is not very easy to create a hodgepodge of confusing headlines and disjointed blocks of text in this way.

The biggest disadvantage of this type of structure is that you do need something on the HTTP server (or connected to it) to create these pages. A dynamically created page with minimal data—perhaps a message like, "Thank you, Maureen, for your comments"—can be generated by a Perl script with a single parameter ("Maureen"). However, more complex pages such as the one described here require a database with at least the power of FileMaker Pro, Microsoft Access, or SQL Server.

A secondary disadvantage is the complement of the by-product described previously. Some HTML-centric Web designers prefer to hand-tune each page. There is no doubt that such hand-tuning can yield superlative results; however, you need to decide what the cost is and whether or not you are willing to bear it.

Interacting with the User's Computer

Finally, you can extend the basic HTTP/HTML functionality by causing a script or program to run on the user's computer. There are three ways in which you can do this:

1. Your HTML pages can contain scripts that a user's browser can interpret and run. In these cases, the code (in JavaScript, Visual Basic, or other languages) is downloaded as part of the page. It is typically hidden from browsers that do not support scripting by embedding it in comments on the pages.

2. Your page can cause a program to start to run on the user's computer and can interact with it. Java, for example, is executed in something called a Java Virtual Machine. The Virtual Machine runs on the user's com-

puter and processes Java byte code (semicompiled code) that is downloaded on a Web page.

3. You can download a document that is processed by a helper application or a plug-in to your browser. This means simply that if you download a document such as a spreadsheet, your browser and operating system will collaborate to cause it to be opened by Microsoft Excel or whatever spreadsheet program you have selected.

Why You May Want to Do This

In these ways, you can cause actions to happen on a user's computer that are beyond the scope of HTML and a browser. For example, just as the previous section described interaction with a database on the server, you can cause data to be downloaded as part of a Web page and then have it stored on the user's computer in a file or database. These two functionalities (called server-side programming and client-side programming) let you exploit fully the capabilities of all the computers that are available to you and the user.

What You Need to Do This

The first item on your checklist is that you must know whether the resources you require are available to your users. When it comes to server-side programming, this is easy: you need to know what one computer installation (your ISP or HTTP server) contains. In this case, you need to know what your users have.

For a corporate intranet, this is simple. In the outside world, however, it is quite complex. Two areas can provide severe limitations:

1. Not all browsers support the links that you need. Although all modern browsers support scripting, plug-ins, and the tools that you will need, many people are running years-old versions of browsers. Forcing people to use a certain browser or certain version of a browser is not easy. Other forces are pushing them

(for similar reasons) to use different browsers and different versions. (Frequently, people are unable to use the latest versions because they break other applications that they use.)

2. Users can turn off scripts, plug-ins, and other links that you may need. Thus, even if they have the capabilities, they may not be accessible.

It is tempting to think that you are just asking your users to make a minor change to their environment. However, remember that you are likely not to be the only one making such a request.

Pros and Cons

The advantages of using resources on a user's computer include not only that you can go beyond basic HTML functionality but also that you can get performance that is not possible with relatively low-speed Internet connections.

The major disadvantage is the fact that you begin to require quite a specific configuration on users' computers: this may or may not be achievable (or maintainable).

The Next Generation: XHTML and Cascading Style Sheets

HTML has two areas of weakness:

1. It is built on SGML, which is quite powerful but equally complex.

2. Additions to HTML have made it increasingly complex.

A further difficulty—not directly attributed to HTML—is that its implementations in editors and browsers have tended to be generous with regard to syntactical ambiguities. This means that HTML that works in one environment does not always work the same way in another environment; there are also many tricks that experienced HTML coders know—tricks made necessary by inconsistent implementations.

XHTML 1 is a reformulation of HTML 4. It addresses all of these issues.

XML

Extensible markup language (XML) is a subset of SGML; version 1.0 was adopted as a recommendation by the W3C (World Wide Web Consortium) on February 10, 1998. Unlike SGML, XML was designed specifically for the Internet. It minimizes optional features and is designed for processing both by people who may view the files and by software. Like SGML, it allows you to define document types—such as HTML or XHTML. (You do not write directly in XML in most cases.)

Because XML has been simplified from the full range of SGML, and because it is targeted at the Web with its assortment of browsers, it is at the same time more flexible and more rigid than SGML and HTML. The increased flexibility comes from the fact that it is easy to define new document types in XML; elements specific to certain businesses (such as <address> tags) can be defined easily.

Its increased rigidity comes from a tightening of standards, most particularly in the fact that it is case sensitive. This is a long-standing argument in the programming world: should the variable CLIENT be the same as or different from Client or client or ClIeNT? Feelings run quite high (and have for decades). Without taking sides on what should be the case, it is sufficient to remember that XML is case sensitive.

XHTML

XHTML is HTML 4 reformulated to use XML as its document definition language. (HTML uses SGML directly; XHTML uses XML directly and SGML indirectly.) As browsers and editors become XHTML aware, you will be able to write in XHTML. If your HTML is well formed, the difference between HTML and XHTML is minimal.

You should write (and have your Web pages written) either in XHTML or in well-formed HTML. Well-formed HTML has the advantages of being easier to read, more consistent in its display in a variety of browsers, and correct. The easiest way to make certain that your HTML is well formed is to use HTML Tidy by Dave Raggett, the W3C lead for HTML, Math and Voice Browsers. It is available at http://www.w3.org/People/Raggett/tidy/. Versions for most operating systems are available; in addition, in can be integrated into a variety of editing programs—your HTML/XHTML editor may already include it.

There are several important changes in XHTML from HTML that you should remember:

- **Case matters.** All XHTML element and attribute names are in lowercase. (Thus you have <p> tags, not <P> tags.)

- **End tags are required or the start tag must end with a /.** No longer can you insert a line break with <br>; it must be either
</br> or <br/>.

- **Attribute values must be in quotes.** In HTML, you could write `align=right` or `ALIGN=right` or any combination of capitalization. In XHTML, you must write `align="right"` instead.

The other changes have to do with tightening up rules—you cannot get away with some of the misplaced tags that you could in the past.

This tightening up affects sloppy HTML coders. The sloppiest tend to be automatic HTML generators—particularly those in word processing programs that allow you a Save As HTML option. If you are generating HTML pages automatically in this way, run HTML Tidy.

What You Need to Do

XML and XHTML are coming. Because of the enormous installed base of existing browsers, this change will be slow for many people. However, as new computers and browsers proliferate, people will be using XHTML. In addition, specific pages will rely on XML and XHTML—those computers and browsers will be updated sooner. (Within some large organizations, XML is already a serious tool.)

Make certain that your HTML pages are compatible with XHTML. This means making certain that they adhere strictly to HTML rules in most cases. Nothing that you do to make them compatible with XHTML will make them incompatible with HTML. Thus, get in the habit of being a stickler for those syntactical elements that differ between the two protocols.

The one thing you should not do is to get involved in discussions about the merits of HTML, XHTML, and so forth. HTML is today's de facto standard; tightening up on the syntax (which is all you need to do for now) is just good housekeeping.

Note that most pages today are HTML pages; XHTML pages are starting to emerge. Rather than kill the trees necessary to support the phrase "HTML or XHTML page," the author uses the term HTML to include HTML and XHTML unless XHTML is specifically excluded.

Cascading Style Sheets

In addition to XML and XHTML, other new directions in Web page implementation exist. One of the most important is Cascading Style Sheets (CSS).

Cascading Style Sheets let you split the Web page formatting across two files: one is a fairly standard HTML file, and the other is a style sheet file. This lets you define styles (as you would in a word processor) to be defined to specific elements on the Web page. You can change the look of the page by substituting different style sheets; you do not have to modify the HTML—the content—in order to change its appearance.

Style sheets are very powerful; they help to arrange the morass of low-level formatting (alignment, italics, fonts, and so forth) into higher level structures (headlines, body text, field names). Not all browsers support Cascading Style Sheets, so you need to be careful with relying on them.

Summary

This chapter focuses on three critical areas for the Web-based enterprise: basic structural issues, communications, and the future directions of HTML. In each area, you need to know what your options are and how to choose the directions for your site to take.

Whereas the first decade of the Web was marked by rapid developments of the most basic kind (consensus as to terms such as "webmaster" and "shopping cart," the introduction of frames, and advanced formatting using specific fonts and style sheets), the next years are likely to build on that framework. So the choices that you make today are likely to be able to stay in effect for some time: there is simply too much content on the Web using the existing technologies for massive sea changes to occur as was the case in the mid-1990s.

Looking at a Web Page

6

Although some people shudder at the thought, in most cases it really is not necessary to learn how to create Web pages from scratch. It is sufficient to be able to look at an existing page, decide how you want to modify it, and know just enough to make those changes. Few programmers or Web page designers actually start with a blank screen; in most cases, they start either with a shell or with something that is similar and which they can modify.

(Of course, in modifying existing code, you have to be careful that you do not copy code which is not yours to copy.)

Thus, this chapter provides you with an introduction to what a Web page looks like—both from the user's point of view (that is, on the

119

screen) and from the designer's point of view (how it is coded). The sections of this chapter are:

- *"Parts of Web Pages." This is a breakdown of the visual aspects of a Web page. It is not at the HTML level: it is at the level that designers and managers need to discuss.*

- *"Characteristics of Web Pages." Web pages can be categorized in many ways. The taxonomy outlined here lets you identify characteristics of Web pages that matter in their design and implementation.*

- *"Defining a Web Page's Function." Finally, this part of the chapter shows you how to identify what a Web page should be doing. This helps in its design and implementation.*

This taxonomy of Web page parts helps you evaluate pages—both those that exist and those that you may be planning. You have a framework in which to discuss and compare pages. (All too often, these discussions either do not take place or take place in the rarefied atmosphere of vague theories and amorphous concepts such as "taste" or "like/dislike." Pinning these issues down can help you to produce effective Web pages quickly.)

Before launching into your Web page registry, be sure to read the next chapter as well as this one: it may inspire you to rule out—or rule in—certain parts and characteristics identified here.

Parts of Web Pages

HTML defines parts of pages (such as their head and body elements). As used here, "parts" refers to visible aspects of the page. Some correspond to HTML elements; others are simply content. Not all Web pages have all of these elements (nor should they).

The primary parts of a Web page are:

- Title

- Site identifier
- References
- Ads
- Heading
- Site navigation aids
- Content
- Action buttons
- Contact information
- Copyright information
- Creation and modification dates
- Versions and cycles
- Author and owner
- Counters and logs

This may appear a pedantic taxonomy, but spend a few moments browsing the Web at random. You will find pages with no titles—or incorrect titles. If you use a search engine, you may find the answer to your question, "How did Claverack get its name?" but the provenance of the page with the answer is a mystery. (You may be able to wend your way to some clue as to the provider by stepping up the URL to the domain name, but that does not always help.)

Even worse, if you decide that you would like to quote the Claverack description, the absence of an author or copyright information puts you in a very serious bind: the page is by default copyrighted (in the United States) due to its publication. However, in the absence of an identified copyright owner, you have no right to use it and no way to obtain that right. This does not mean that you can go ahead and use the page as your own: rather, it means that it is totally off limits to all reproduction.

An example page is shown in Figures 6-1 (top) and 6-2 (bottom). (There is additional content on the page between these two figures.) It is used to illustrate the parts of a Web page.

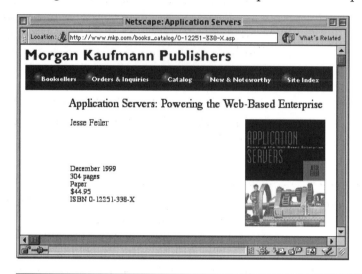

FIGURE 6-1. Application Servers Page (top)

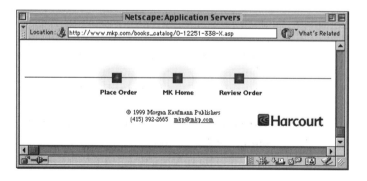

FIGURE 6-2. Application Servers Page (bottom)

Title	The title is "Application Servers." This is an HTML element (the <title> element). It is used by browsers to identify the page in the window's frame. (It may also be used in bookmarks and history lists.) The title element is frequently wrong. This happens when someone copies a template or an existing page and makes the few modifications needed to turn it into a new page. All too often, the title is skipped in this process. It should take you about 2 minutes to find a mistitled page as you surf the Web. Not even the best sites are immune from this problem.

Site Identifier	The site is "Morgan Kaufmann Publishers." You can tell this because it is prominently featured at the top of the page. This is a corporate design feature: the font and its color are not subject to the vagaries of browser interpretation. It is an image. It cannot be resized or reshaped. A site identifier is often presented as a logo or graphic of this sort. Also, it is frequently a link to the site's home page.

The site name is not your domain name: it refers to the virtual place that users understand they are visiting (see "What Is the Virtual Web Site Place?" starting on page 45). It can be your entire site, or it can be a subsite such as your online sales site, a separate investor relations site, and so forth.

On composite pages, this is often presented in a relatively static frame.

References	A reference is a logo or text (often with a link behind it) that provides additional information to the user about the provenance, ownership, and standards of a site. In this case, the Harcourt logo at the lower right of Figure 6-2 is a reference. Clicking on it takes you to the Harcourt site—www.har-

court.com. The relationship between Morgan Kaufmann and Harcourt is described on both the Morgan Kaufmann and Harcourt home pages: "Morgan Kaufmann is a Division of Academic Press, a Harcourt Science and Technology Company."

On composite pages, this is often presented in a relatively static frame.

In addition to ownership, other types of references may be logos of ratings or security services that vouch for the site and its technology, trade associations, or other related organizations. A frequent reference is the logo of and link to the company that has prepared the Web site or its content. Other frequent references are to the products used to support the Web site—Web servers, databases, HTML authoring tools, and the like.

Ads

There are no ads shown on this page. However, they function to all intents and purposes just like references—which is what they are. They are related organizations. Ads usually consist of graphics with links behind them—just like references. They are usually inserted onto a site dynamically so that different ads appear for different users at different times. Except for this, they behave just like references.

Heading

The heading is "Application Servers: Powering the Web-Based Enterprise" (the title of the book described on this page).

Telling the difference among the title, heading, and site identifier is one of those things that humans do almost without thinking. The title is the easiest to identify: it is the HTML <title> element and it appears as the window title. The heading of the page uniquely identifies the page (or rather, it should). The site identifier is a reference to the site on which the page is found; it typically appears on many pages rather than just on one (as the heading does). No matter where on the page the site identifier and the heading appear, it is usually not difficult to differentiate them. If it is, you need to redesign the layout.

Site Navigation Aids

These let you move around the site. In this case, they are the buttons shown at the top of the page—"Booksellers," "Orders & Inquiries,", "Catalog," "New & Noteworthy," and "Site Index."

Site navigation aids are typically implemented in any of four ways:

1. They can be ordinary text-based links.

2. They can be images with links associated with them (the case here). If the images are all of the same height, they can be placed on the same line so that they appear to be a solid bar. You do this by placing them within a nobreak element (<nobr> and <nobr/>). Note that <nobr> is not a standard W3C element although it is supported by both Netscape Navigator and Microsoft Internet Explorer. Here is a snippet of such code. (It is a variation on part of the page shown in these figures.)

```
<CENTER>
<P>
<nobr>
<A HREF="../booksellers.htm">
    <IMG SRC="../booksellers.gif" ALT="Booksellers" WIDTH=90
        HEIGHT=39 BORDER=0 ALIGN=bottom></A>
<A HREF="../books_orders_inquiries.htm">
    <IMG SRC="../orders.gif" ALT="Orders &amp; Inquiries"
        WIDTH=120 HEIGHT=39 BORDER=0 ALIGN=bottom></A>
<</nobr></P></CENTER>
```

3. They can be an image map. This is a single image with a variety of hot areas, each of which has its own link associated with it. An image map consists of a map definition—the coordinates and links for each area—and then an IMG element that associates that map

with a graphic. A typical image map description looks like this:

```
<MAP NAME=map1>
    <AREA SHAPE=rect COORDS="16,128,249,219"
    HREF="http://www.philmontmill.com/filemaker/index.html"
        TARGET="_blank">
    <AREA SHAPE=rect COORDS="14,19,253,90"
    HREF="http://www.philmontmill.com/people/index.html"
        TARGET=baseframe>
    <AREA SHAPE=default HREF="http://www.philmontmill.com"
        TARGET="_top">
</MAP>
<IMG USEMAP="#map1" SRC="/psm.logo.JPG" WIDTH=269 HEIGHT=273>
```

4. They can be scripted navigation aids that are created with JavaScript or ActiveX controls. These are the navigation aids in which colors change as you move the mouse over various areas. (Chapter 13 of *Database-Driven Web Sites*, "Scripting for Database Applications," contains details and some example code.)

On composite pages, this is often presented in a relatively static frame.

Content

The body of the page—text, graphics, links, and everything else—is the content. This material is presented only on this page; it is not duplicated.

Action Buttons

Examples of these are shown in Figure 6-2. These are similar to site navigation aids, but they are normally specific to the content of the page.

"Place Order" and "Review Order" on this page are such examples. The middle button—"MK Home"—could be considered a site navigation aid; however, its placement with the action buttons suggests a different interpretation—"finished with this page." That is a page-specific action.

Contact Information	Many pages provide contact information for feedback and questions. Sometimes a distinction is drawn between feedback about the Web page itself and other feedback (such as ordering products). In this case, the feedback information consists of a contact phone number and an e-mail address (mkp@mkp.com). Note that providing both an Internet contact—e-mail or a Web page—and a phone or physical address for contact makes it possible for people who may be uncomfortable with one technology or another to reach you. On composite pages, this is often presented in a relatively static frame.
Copyright Information	Each page should have copyright information on it. That information should (at a minimum) provide the date of publication and the owner of the copyright. The absence of copyright information does not mean that the material is uncopyrighted or is in the public domain, although some people may surmise that. If you are specifically donating material to the public domain or if you allow certain types of user, that should be made clear. On composite pages, this is often presented in a relatively static frame.
Creation and Modification Dates	Although the page shown here does not provide this information, frequently pages provide their creation and modification dates. This helps internal maintenance; it also can help people to know how fresh the information is.

This is one reason why such information is sometimes not provided: it can be obvious that a page is 2, 3, or even 10 years old. If the page contains a scene from *Hamlet*, its age does not really matter; however, in many cases, Web users believe that recent is better.

Note that creation and modification dates can be entered as comments in the source code of the pages. You can also rely on the timestamps generated automatically for the files by the operating system. Each strategy has its drawbacks. Manually updating the creating and modification dates in comments is prone to error (and sins of omission); relying on the operating system's timestamps exposes you to problems when a computer's internal clock is set incorrectly.

Versions and Cycles

Pages can have version and cycle numbers; these are usually written in a format such as 1.5 or 27.3 where the first number is the version and the second is the cycle. As with creation and modification dates, this information may be stored in comments inside the page.

A common strategy is to provide a version for a particular iteration of a Web site (or subsite) and to provide cycles for individual pages. For example, the first version of your site might be version 1, and all pages would be identified as 1.0. As modifications are made to individual pages, some would wind up with version information such as 1.3 or (in the case of frequently updated pages) 1.427.

Page Identifier

An identifier for each page makes it easy to locate the page in your Web page registry and other records. One common strategy is to compose identifiers by using subsite information to group pages. Thus, a page identifier of 1.4.5 and another of 1.4.6 could be generated for adjacent pages.

The problem with such complex numbering schemes is that the scheme is vulnerable to the common changes in the organization of Web sites. Do not use the page identifier for anything other than identification. Use unique numbers (these can be generated automatically by a spreadsheet or database). With this strategy, page 37 is page 37 no matter whether it is part of subsite 4 or subsite 400. Identifiers (whether of database records or of Web pages) are at their best when they are meaningless.

Author and Owner	Usually not shown on the page, the author and owner are important pieces of information for your Web page registry.
Counters and Logs	Visible or not, counter and logs can be part of a page. You can use them to track your page's usage; you can also use them to demonstrate to people how popular (hence useful) your page is to others. As noted previously, counters and logs are not always accurate. Not only can they be manipulated (by users as well as by Web page owners), they also are not updated when pages in caches are accessed.

Characteristics of Web Pages

There are no rules for Web pages, other than that they use HTML or XHTML in their coding. You can categorize pages in any way that you want—by background color, alphabetized by page titles, or by size.

The purpose of characterizing Web pages is to know what features they contain that matter—both to users and to you as a developer, maintainer, and manager. In addition, as with identifying the parts of Web pages, identifying the characteristics of Web pages gives you a common vocabulary and a way to discuss and compare Web pages.

Not all characteristics listed here will apply to your pages. As part of developing your site (and subsites), you should review these characteristics and make a high-level decision on which ones will be banished from the site, which will be required, and which will be optional. Once you have made these decisions, you can track the remaining characteristics for the pages on the site.

For example, you may decide that all pages on your site will be in English (or French or Portuguese or Japanese). If your organization is located in France, Brazil, or Japan, such a decision would be appropriate. And, in such a case, there is no reason to track the language of each individual page. However, if your organization is international or is located in a region with multiple languages, the language characteristics become important for each page on the site.

Likewise, you may decide that for security reasons no page on your site will use ActiveX controls. Again, that simplifies matters: there is no point knowing whether any individual page contains ActiveX controls since none of them will.

Characteristics for Users

It is easy to make a list of characteristics that matter to users: look in the Preferences or Properties windows of browsers and see what features a user can turn off. These characteristics are those that you cannot rely on in Web pages.

Characteristics for You

Characteristics that matter to you are those that require you to maintain skills or software to develop or maintain them.

Languages

Unless your site consists only of images, it has one or more languages for its text. Languages use various character sets for their display; accordingly, your language choices are actually combinations of languages and representations.

If your site is multilingual, you need to decide whether to use a separate page for each language or whether each page has two (or more) sections. And in the latter case, you need to further consider whether the two (or more) sections are equal; in other words, does one summarize the other.

Images

Users can turn off image loading in their browser. If they do, none of your graphics is displayed. People tend to do this if they have slow connections to the Internet or if they are using devices that do not support images. These devices include very old dumb terminals in public libraries as well as very new cell phones and other Internet appliances that have minimal if any image support.

Vision-impaired people also may not have access to images on their Web pages. Speech synthesis software just cannot synthesize an image; and high-magnification monitors work well with text, but magnifying an image to an extreme degree can often make it totally undecipherable.

Furthermore, consider the use of images that contain text (such as logos, site maps, scanned documents, and so forth). When text is displayed as part of an embedded image, it loses its textual characteristics and replaces them with the raw pixels of an image. Thus, an image containing the word "llama" is not going to be found by a site search tool.

Each of these reasons—connection speed, device capabilities, vision impairment, and embedded text—can limit the usefulness of images. You may want to make your site specifically accessible to the image-impaired user. Among other things, that means making certain that the alt attribute of each image element is set. (The alt attribute is a string that is displayed in place of the image if the image cannot be displayed; it can also be spoken by speech synthesis software). Other accommodations for people who do not see images on their Web pages include forgoing the use of image maps (or duplicating their navigational facilities with text-based tools).

Page Size

Web pages should contain text and images that can flow appropriately as the browser window is resized. Large images cannot flow. If your logo or navigational image map is particularly wide or tall, you set a minimum page width or height: users whose windows are smaller than that minimum must use scroll bars to see the entire page.

The advent of new devices such as cell phones with Internet access is shaking things up. Designers have assumed that monitors and viewing areas will only get bigger with the passage of time. Suddenly, viewing areas can get much smaller than they ever did before.

This is a characteristic that should be set at the site level. You may have several site-wide page sizes that can be used, or you may enforce a single size.

Bandwidth

Pages with high-quality graphics, audio, video, or long scripts require a longer time to load than purely text-based pages. You may optimize a page for dial-up connections or for high-speed T1 access.

Style Sheets

As noted in the previous chapter, style sheets are a way to separate the physical formatting of pages from their content. Most modern browsers support style sheets; however, this is a feature that users can turn off, so you must include it in your choices about whether or not a page uses it.

Cookies

Cookies are used to store information on the user's computer. They are under the control of the user (and sometimes of the user's network manager). Typical cookie settings allow the user to:

- Refuse all cookies.

- Respond yes or no to each cookie storage request.

- Accept cookies that are visible only to the HTTP server placing them.

If your page uses cookies, plan for what to do if it cannot store (or retrieve) its cookie. Also, if you set cookies, remember to make that clear in your privacy statement. (See "Privacy" on page 142.)

Scripting Languages

The first choice here is to determine whether you will use scripts on a page. If you do, you must choose what language(s) to use—JavaScript, TCL, PerlScript, VBScript, and so forth. Note, too, that users can turn off scripts, so your page may just sit there. You need either to provide nonscripting alternatives or to make it clear to the user that scripting must be turned on.

The noscript HTML element can be helpful. The content of the noscript element is displayed if scripting is not supported by the user's browser (or if it has been turned off); it is also displayed if a specific scripting language that has been used previously on the page is not supported. Typically, the noscript element contains a simple message such as the following example:

```
This page requires JavaScript. Use a browser that supports Jav-
aScript and make certain that your scripting Preferences and
```

```
Properties are set properly.
```

Links are provided to pages listing appropriate browsers and settings. The HTML code follows (if you use it, you will need to substitute the names of the pages you create with the lists of browsers and settings):

```
<noscript>
<P>This page requires JavaScript. Use a
    <A HREF="okbrowsers.html">
        browser that supports JavaScript</A>
    and make certain that your scripting
    <A HREF="settingscriptingprefs.html">
        Preferences and Properties</A>
    are set properly.
</P>
</noscript>
```

This, too, can be a site-wide decision. You can place this snippet of code on every page that uses scripts, or you can place it on your home page. If scripts are used on many pages on your site, the home page is a good location; if they are used infrequently, just place the warning where it is needed.

Programming Languages

If your pages use ActiveX controls or Java, programs will need to run on your users' computers. You can also cause programs to run by downloading files that need to be processed by helper applications (such as Acrobat Reader). Keep track of what you are doing. Make certain that the user knows what additional tools are required (either for the site or on a page-by-page basis). In addition, try to minimize the diversity of programming languages so that you can maintain the expertise to manage your site.

Downloading Files

Files that are downloaded from your site may need helper applications to be processed. Remember that downloading is not always feasible for every user. They can turn off downloading features in their browsers. Furthermore, firewalls and corporate security may prevent downloads. And if this is not enough, remember that downloading a gigabyte file is not always feasible over slow lines, and downloading a file to a cell phone is a neat trick.

If a page allows the user the option to download a file, that should be noted. If a page automatically invokes a download, that should be noted—and avoided in most cases.

Ratings

Ratings (often reflecting sex, nudity, violence, and language) are often implemented to help people screen the pages that they, their families, and their colleagues at work view. This area is evolving rapidly; however, if it is relevant to you, you will need to rate each area of your site.

One of the major organizations involved in this field is the Internet Content Rating Association (ICRA).[1] Its original members include AOL Europe; British Telecom; Bertelsmann Foundation; Cable & Wireless; Demon Internet (UK); Deutsche Telekom Online Service; Electric Network Consortium, Japan; EuroISPA; IBM; Internet Watch Foundation; Microsoft; Software and Information Industries Association; and UUNet. The system involves an interactive rating process that you step through, specifying attributes of the page, site, or subsite that you are rating. At the end of the process, the system generates a meta-tag to be placed in the head element of your HTML page.

The meta-tag adheres to the World Wide Web Consortium's Platform for Internet Content Selection (PICS) specification.[2] It can be read and interpreted by most browsers; they will screen pages out based on the contents of that tag.

---

1. Its Web site is located at http://www.icra.org.
2. For more information, see http://http://www.w3.org/PICS/.

Depending on your site, its contents, and your users, you may need to rate it with other organizations instead of or in addition to ICRA. Some filtering software and browsers will block pages that have unsatisfactory ratings—or no ratings at all.

The issues of rating and filtering are far from resolved on the Internet. Even the most basic issue—whether to filter out or filter in—does not have a consensus. In practice, it is often not difficult to make certain that your site is seen by people who should see it and avoided by people who should not if you use ratings. The difficult cases are those that involve automatic screening and filtering: those are the cases in which sites about breast cancer have been screened out (because of the word "breast") and in which sites containing synopses of Greek dramas have been screened out (due to violent language).

Obligatory Hardware and Software

Some hardware and software may be obligatory to view your page. You may need support for audio or video, and if your page needs to interact with an operating system, it may require users to use only that operating system.

Once again, make certain that you know these issues before the page is deployed. If it works only on the Macintosh (or on Windows), the statement that "all our users have a Mac (or Windows)" should be known to be true.

Recommended Hardware and Software

There is a less stringent category of hardware and software that help pages work well but are not required. (This is frequently the case with sound: better speakers will make it sound better, but tinny ones will work.)

Composite Pages (Frames)

A page can consist of a single HTML file. It can also consist of two or more frames, each of which contains an HTML file. Each frame is loaded separately. This technique allows you to mix pages from various sites and servers. It is also a very practical way in which to implement navigation aids.

The following example is from the HTML 4.01 Specification W3C Recommendation 24 December 1999; it demonstrates how frames can be set up: [3]

```
<!DOCTYPE HTML PUBLIC "-//W3C//DTD HTML 4.01 Frameset//EN"
  "http://www.w3.org/TR/html4/frameset.dtd">
<HTML>
<HEAD>
   <TITLE>A simple frameset document</TITLE>
</HEAD>
<FRAMESET cols="20%, 80%">
   <FRAMESET rows="100, 200">
      <FRAME src="contents_of_frame1.html">
      <FRAME src="contents_of_frame2.gif">
   </FRAMESET>
   <FRAME src="contents_of_frame3.html">
<NOFRAMES>
   <P>This frameset document contains:
   <UL>
      <LI><A href="contents_of_frame1.html">
         Some neat contents</A>
      <LI><IMG src="contents_of_frame2.gif"
         alt="A neat image">
      <LI><A href="contents_of_frame3.html">
         Some other neat contents</A>
   </UL>
</NOFRAMES>
</FRAMESET>
</HTML>
```

The resulting page is shown schematically in Figure 6-3. Here is how the code breaks down. There are, in fact, two sets of

3. The document is available at http://www.w3.org/TR/ html4/present/frames.html#h-16.5. It is copyright ©1997-1999 W3C® (MIT, INRIA, Keio) All Rights Reserved. http:// www.w3.org/Consortium/Legal/.

frames on this page. The first frameset consists of two columns: the first is 20% of the width of the page, the second is 80% of the width. The first column is then split vertically, with the top part (frame 1) being 100 pixels deep and the second part (frame 2) being 200 pixels deep. Finally, a noframes element is shown. This text is displayed on browsers that do not support frames. (By the end of the 1990s, this was a relatively infrequent occurrence. However, with the advent of handheld Internet devices, the situation has emerged again as a possibility for some sites.)

In fact, this structure is that shown in a figure in the previous chapter (see "Philmont Software Mill Home Page" on page 107). In the upper left corner—frame 1—you find navigation aids to other parts of the site. In the lower left corner—frame 2—are navigation aids to other pages within the same subsite. This frame also contains links to the site's copyright and privacy information pages. The contents of pages appear in frame 3.

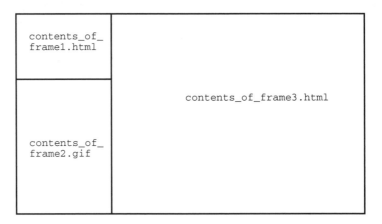

FIGURE 6-3. Frames Example

This structure is very popular on Web sites because it means that much of the site-specific information can appear in frames that do not need to be reloaded. The alternative is to place links to other parts of the site on each page.

Frames are described in detail in most HTML references. However, there are four attributes that you need to know about to use them efficiently on a site; you can implement the basic structure shown here with little more. The four attributes that you need to know about are frame borders, scrollbars, sizes, and names.

Frame Borders

The frameborder attribute specifies the width of the border around each frame. The one number that you need to know is 0—if you set the frameborder to 0, there will be no frame. Users will not know that there is a frame there, since everything will appear as one page. You can add this attribute to the frameset tag as shown here:

```
<FRAMESET cols="20%, 80%" frameborder=0>
```

Scrolling

...except if there are scrollbars. If the page displayed in the frame is bigger than the size of the frame, by default a browser will put scrollbars into the frame. In a navigation area, this often looks strange. To prevent scrollbars appearing, you set scrolling=no, and you make certain that the frame is big enough for its contents.

In addition to adding frameborder, you can add scrolling to the frameset tag as follows:

```
<FRAMESET cols="20%, 80%" frameborder=0 scrolling = no>
```

Set scrolling=no for navigation frames; for the main frame in a window, omit the attribute or set it to yes.

Frame Sizes

You can size a frame in one of three ways:

1. You can specify the number of pixels in its width or height.

2. You can specify the percentage of the window's width or height that it can take up.

3. You can specify that it take up what space is left after a fixed-size frame is displayed.

Here is how it works for a typical page. If you are using one or two frames at the left for navigation aids, you know the size of those frames. You usually place an image map or other image in the frame's page; if you use text, you use a small amount. You specify that frame's size in pixels: the exact size of the image. You then use a * to specify the width of the other frame on the page.

In the example given previously, the first frameset consists of the column on the left (which itself contains frames 1 and 2). You could rewrite that code as follows:

```
<FRAMESET cols="100, *" frameborder=0 scrolling = no>
```

This will make both frames 1 and 2 to be 100 pixels wide; frame 3 (the second column of the frameset) will be whatever space is left in the window. As the user resizes the window, frame 3 will be resized; frames 1 and 2 will be unchanged.

Names

The final attribute that you normally need to set is a name for each frame. This is set in the frame tag. Again, using the example shown previously, here is how you could name the first of the three frames.

```
<FRAME src="contents_of_frame1.html" name="frame1">
```

As part of the href tag, you can specify the frame in which the link will be displayed. Your choices are:

• TARGET="_blank" This will cause the link to be opened in a new window.

• TARGET="_self" This will cause the link to be opened in the same frame as the link.

- TARGET="_parent" This will cause the link to be opened in the frame to which the current frame belongs. In many cases, this behavior is confusing to users.

- TARGET="_top" This will cause the link to be opened in the outermost window—all frames will be eliminated (unless the linked page has frames).

- TARGET=framename This causes the link to be opened in the frame identified. This is how you let a navigation aid image map (on the left in this example) open a link in the main part of the window. To do this, the frame for the main part of the window must be named. A common name is "base." In such cases, links in navigation aids at the left all target "base."

Off-site links generally target either _top or _blank. If you omit the target, you will open the link in the same frame as the link; this is how you can get frames within frames within frames. It is normally very annoying.

Using frames can drastically decrease the time it takes to load pages (less information needs to be loaded and imaged). It can also significantly reduce maintenance costs. When first developed, frames were often misused; people did not know how to use them in an intuitive way. As a result, they got a bad reputation in some quarters. Today, though, they are commonly used.

Setting Up Frames

If you use frames, you can use them to implement navigation aids, boilerplate text and links (such as to copyright and privacy statements), and to present a logo. This takes a big burden off your content pages.

If you use frames in this way, start out with a plan that includes caching information. Logos and navigation aids can frequently be cached for long periods of time. This significantly improves performance and decreases network loads.

Caching Information	Although not visible on the page (it is in the HTTP header), caching information is always a critical part of a page. Make no mistake: caching information is always present. If you omit it, you lose control over how your page is treated by the various caches on the Internet. (Refer to "Caching" starting on page 88 for more information on caching and how to implement it.)
Security	Pages may have special security considerations. If a page uses security features, you need to identify them and make certain that they are implemented—and that they remain implemented during revisions to the page. Security has a variety of performance consequences (such as the fact that secure pages normally cannot be cached). From the perspective of the site, you need to make certain that you use consistent security mechanisms on all of your pages. Finally, note that security implementations sometimes overlap with previous characteristics if they require users to use certain browsers or versions of browsers; they also may interact by requiring additional software to be installed at the user's site. [4]
Privacy	Related to security, privacy is a characteristic of a page in two ways:

1. If a page collects information—explicitly or implicitly—from an identifiable user, you have a privacy issue. Thus, page counters normally do not trigger privacy issues, whereas forms with a name and/or e-mail address always do. However, page counters that

---

4. For further information, see Chapter 10, "Security and Application Servers," in *Application Servers: Powering the Web-Based Enterprise*.

also collect information on a user's IP address probably will trigger privacy concerns.

2. If the page presents information about an individual or organization that is not publicly known, privacy concerns are raised.

If privacy is an issue on a page, that page should have a link to your privacy statement. If your site's home page has such a link, that can be acceptable, but if people can get to an individual page without going through the home page, the per-page links are preferable.

Site Awareness

If you have navigation aids to areas of your site (its home page, copyright and privacy statements, and so forth), your page has site awareness. A change to the site layout—with no change to the page in question—can break the page.

This is a characteristic of Web pages that is critically important for maintenance. In addition to navigation aids, which tend to be clustered in an image map or other block, individual links can exhibit site awareness. Look at these links and you will see how site awareness works.

This link is to a page on the Internet—it can be on your site or on someone else's.

```
For more information on W3C, click
    <A HREF="http://www.w3c.org">here</A>.
```

The following link is to a page on your site and in the same directory as the page on which the link is placed:

```
For our privacy statement, click
    <A HREF="privacy.html">here</A>.
```

Note that the HREF attribute contains only the resource name; the scheme (http:) and host name are omitted. Moving either the page with the link or the other page to another directory will break this link.

The link that follows also has site awareness. It links to a file that is in the directory above the one in which the page resides (the ../ before the resource name means to look in the enclosing directory).

```
For our copyright statement, click
    <A HREF="../copyright.html">here</A>.
```

Similarly, this link looks in a directory within the directory in which the page resides:

```
For our mission statement, click
    <A HREF="/policies/mission.html">here</A>.
```

If you use navigation aids to your site, each page on which they are placed is site aware; this is normally good for users, and it creates a real sense of the "place" where your site is in cyberspace. Unfortunately, if those navigation aids are physically placed on each page, you will need to update them whenever the site changes.

If you have navigation aids on each page (rather than placing them in a frame), recognize that they will change over time. You can construct relatively unchanging pages that are gateways to sections of your site. Use these in the navigation aids rather than starting a constant flood of changes to each page on the site whenever a page moves or is renamed.

Using a full URL complete with host name might appear to be a safer route than using relative URLs which omit the host name. However, this is not always the case. If you use relative URLs, you can move the entire site from one directory to another and have it continue to work. This is critical if you have a variety of environments to develop and test your site in.

Content

The last characteristic of a page is its content. This is often the first (and last) characteristic about which people think. It is the most important, but unless all of the other relevant characteristics are identified and managed, your content will disappear or be muddied in its message.

Defining a Web Page's Function

It is sometimes surprising that site coordinators and Web page authors are not clear what the function of each Web page is. A site (or subsite) is usually fairly easy to identify in this regard; however, each page has its own function that contributes to the site's objective.

Defining a page's function is usually not too hard at the start. However, as pages remain on your site and are updated, sometimes the accretions hide the original objective.

Defining a Web page's function is one of the first steps you need to take in developing the page. The process is described at the end of this chapter because it builds on the terminology presented earlier in this chapter and in preceding chapters.

There are three basic Web page functions:

1. **Informational**. These Web pages present information.

2. **Interactive**. These pages ask for input from the user, accept it (possibly with edits), and then transmit it to the server.

3. **Transactional**. Transactional pages are part of multi-page processes. They can be informational (presenting a message such as "Thank you for your order") or interactive ("Please enter your name"). They differ from both informational and interactive pages in that they do not stand alone. In addition, they normally encompass an exchange of value.

Informational Pages

These pages present information. They should contain a complete and logical unit of information—preferably the unit of information that people want. Defining this unit is not always easy.

For example, consider the case of the names and addresses of members of a committee of 50 people. You can place all of that information on a single page—admittedly a fairly long page. In another structure, you can place the names of the 50 people on a single page and have each name link to a separate page with that person's address information (this makes a total of 51 pages).

The choices need to be made based on how people will use the information and how you will maintain it. Above all, it depends on the information itself.

If there is one lesson to be learned in managing data, it is to understand the data. This applies to setting up Web pages, designing databases, laying out brochures, and preparing slide presentations. There is no substitute for getting close to the data: as you work with it, try to update it, try to produce reports, and generally interact with it, you will get to know it in a way that no outsider can. This is an example of how the people in a Web-based enterprise with knowledge of the enterprise itself are critical to the development of successful Web pages.

The parts of Web pages described previously in this chapter have specific roles to play on informational pages. Those roles are outlined in Table 6-1.

Part	Purpose on Informational Pages
Title	Make sure the title for the window reflects the contents.
Site Identifier	Supports the provenance of the information and its authority.
References	Supports the provenance of the information and its authority.
Ads	Optional.
Heading	Identify the information.
Site Navigation Aids	If people can land on this page from the outside (e.g., via search engines), site navigation aids can persuade them to continue their browsing on your site.
Content	Essential for informational pages.
Action Buttons	A "More Info" button is helpful. Feedback buttons ("Did this page answer your question? Yes/no") can be useful if you have the resources to process the information. Do not merely burden the user and clutter the page.
Contact Information	Can provide feedback and be a source of further information coming into the enterprise. Be careful about providing contact information for contentious information.
Copyright Information	Usually essential if you are providing information.
Creation and Modification Dates	Necessary if the information is subject to change.

TABLE 6-1. Parts for Informational Pages

Part	Purpose on Informational Pages
Author and Owner	Optional.
Counters and Logs	Sometimes useful. However, omit for information that must be provided by law or custom. If you will not act on counter information, omit it.

TABLE 6-1. Parts for Informational Pages (Continued)

Interactive Pages

Interactive pages are designed for a single interaction (such as specifying a search term or posting an event to a community calendar). They present the user with either a form or an e-mail link to provide the information. Informational pages often provide feedback links; however, the primary objective of an interactive page is its collection of information.

The parts of Web pages described previously in this chapter have specific roles to play on interactive pages. Those roles are outlined in Table 6-2.

Part	Purpose on Interactive Pages
Title	Make sure the title for the window reflects the contents.
Site Identifier	Clarifies who or what is asking for the information.
References	Clarifies who or what is asking for the information.

TABLE 6-2. Parts for Interactive Pages

Part	Purpose on Interactive Pages
Ads	Optional.
Heading	Identify the information requested.
Site Navigation Aids	A link to the privacy statement should be included (unless it is explicitly on this page).
Content	Gathered from the user.
Action Buttons	"Submit" and "Reset" are standard for forms.
Contact Information	Be careful about providing a secondary way of submitting information. Your carefully prepared form that feeds into a database will be for naught if people e-mail the webmaster with their information.
Copyright Information	Rarely required for input data, but you may want to retain the copyright of your page's wording and its graphics.
Creation and Modification Dates	Necessary. These pages tend to evolve as feedback is received.
Author and Owner	Necessary (but not visible). You need to know who gets the data.
Counters and Logs	Useful only in comparing page hits with actual submissions (i.e., people who decide not to provide the information requested).

TABLE 6-2. Parts for Interactive Pages (Continued)

Transactional   Transactions are multipage sequences that involve the exchange of value (as in e-business). Individual pages within a transaction can be informational or interactive; however, special transactional needs apply to those pages.

The parts of Web pages described previously in this chapter have specific roles to play on transactional pages. Those roles are outlined in Table 6-3 where they differ from those of informational or interactive pages.

Part	Purpose on Transactional Pages
Title	The titles may be dynamic and remain constant for all windows in the transaction; this helps the user know what is going on.
Site Identifier	Clarifies who or what is the counterpart in the transaction.
References	Clarifies who or what is the counterpart in the transaction.
Ads	Optional.
Heading	Identify the transaction in progress.
Site Navigation Aids	Be careful about providing out-of-transaction links during the transaction. You can leave orphaned shopping carts. (Users can abandon the process by moving to another site or shutting down their browser; however, you do not want to encourage them to do so.)
Content	Varies during the transaction.
Action Buttons	Vary by page. "Buy" and "View Cart Contents" are common e-commerce action buttons.

TABLE 6-3. Parts for Transactional Pages

Part	Purpose on Transactional Pages
Contact Information	In providing contacts, try to insert a transaction identifier into a subject line of e-mail messages or into forms. Do not make the user tell the whole story if you can construct it as part of the feedback.
Copyright Information	Rarely required for input data, but you may want to retain the copyright of your page's wording and its graphics.
Creation and Modification Dates	Necessary. These pages tend to evolve as feedback is received.
Author and Owner	Necessary (but not visible). You need to know who gets the data.
Counters and Logs	Useful only in comparing page hits with actual submissions (i.e., people who decide not to provide the information requested).

TABLE 6-3. Parts for Transactional Pages (Continued)

Summary

The parts, characteristics, and functions of Web pages described in this chapter form the basis of a well thought-out site. Starting from the externals (the graphics) does not guarantee that the underpinnings are logical; starting from the logical foundation of a site's pages, however, provides a logic and consistency that will make your site consistent and useful. Furthermore, identifying the parts, characteristics, and functions of Web pages helps you create and manage a Web page registry.

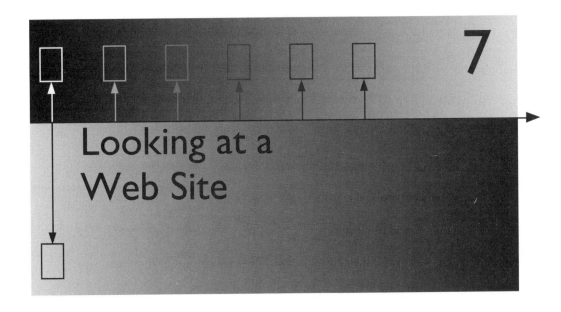

7

Looking at a Web Site

The previous chapter helped you to look at Web pages—their visible parts, characteristics, and functions. This chapter does the same for Web sites. It is divided into three sections:

- *"Scoping a Web Site." Scoping involves the critical decisions you make about what the site will contain and what it will exclude. It is your site definition or mission statement.*

- *"Designing Your Site." This section shows you how to use Web page parts to construct a visually consistent site.*

- *"Structure of Web Sites." Here you will see how to use characteristics of Web pages as well as other structural aspects of the site to create a physically consistent site.*

153

The most important point to note about Web sites is that they do change over time. All too often, people design a Web site as if that were the beginning and end of the process. The Web is littered with such sites: some of them look decidedly quaint these days. Nothing dates faster than an interface that uses the latest bells and whistles: tomorrow's bells and whistles are always better. Focusing on the permanent elements of a Web site—the elements described in this chapter—can help you avoid the problems associated with trendiness and (on the other extreme) quaintness.

Scoping a Web Site

Scoping a site is simply a matter of deciding what the site should include and what it should not include; if a Web site is a virtual place, its scope is the virtual fence surrounding it.

Scoping is critically important to the development, maintenance, and use of your site. When the head of an organization calls in the IT department, the PR division, or an outside consultant and says, "Put up a Web site," every person involved may have a totally different idea of what those five words mean.

The scope of a site encompasses the subject(s) of the site and the types of information it contains. The scope needs to be conveyed to the site owner, the developers and managers, as well as to users. Each group has expectations, and the sooner that they know whether a site will fulfill those expectations, the better it is for everyone. Scoping is all about managing expectations.

Identifying the Subject

This is usually not very difficult: the subjects of Web sites often have direct parallels in the real world. There are sites for individuals, enterprises, political parties, cultural institutions, religions, and movements of all kinds. This parallel makes scoping easy.

Preserving the Subject

As time passes, problems with scope generally crop up. They are all the same sort, but they come in two varieties:

1. Some of the material that belongs on your site winds up being placed in other locations. This is not a matter of duplicate information; rather, it is the case of the original information being posted elsewhere and not being posted (or being posted after the fact) to your site. This often occurs if your update procedures are complex or onerous and people need or want to get their information onto the Web quickly. The result is to dilute your subject: material about XYZ is no longer located only at www.XYZ.com.

2. The same process can happen in reverse. Subject matter that does not belong on your site can be posted there. In this case, it muddies your site's scope. Just what is www.XYZ.com supposed to be about if it also includes information about ABC Corporation? The cause of this is often the same as in the previous case; posting material to www.ABC.com may be burdensome or time consuming and in an informal or formal manner www.XYZ.com resources are borrowed.

Not allowing for easy updates to the site is one of the surest ways to force people to spread onto other sites. "Temporary" solutions involving personal Web pages and free Web sites will abound. On the other hand, the absence of controlled processes for updating will allow your site to become a dumping ground. See "Staging the Changes" starting on page 247 for more information.

Selecting the Data for the Site

Once you have decided what subject(s) the site deals with, you need to decide what data should be posted. This is a more detailed process, and it involves a host of issues. Table 7-1 provides some of the basic types of data and the issues involved in posting or not posting them.

Information	Issues
Contact and Personal Information for People	Many enterprises keep their staff directories confidential to prevent corporate raiding. Schools generally prohibit the publication of students' home contact information.
Contact Information for the Enterprise	Some Web sites provide contact information only for Internet use: no phone or physical address is provided. Others provide physical addresses but no phone contacts.
Links to Off-Site Pages	The two concerns here are that links may go bad (you do not control other sites) and that people may not realize your site does not control the linked information. One solution is to require off-site links to open in a new window (_target="blank").
Purchasing Information	If you produce goods or services, should you sell them directly or should you direct customers to resellers—either by name or with a phrase such as, "See your local battery acid distributor"?
Copyrighted Information	All copyrighted information must be identified. Republication needs to be clearly marked.
Page Creation/ Revision Dates	If too old, these can suggest that the information is stale.
Information Not Available Elsewhere	If clearly identified, this can attract users to your site. Early news or unique items can build traffic.

TABLE 7-1. Types of Information and Issues Relating to Them

A special case of data selection is advertisements: placing ads on your site can be a complex decision. Your two primary concerns are whether the ads clutter your site's message and image and whether they lend your site's imprimatur to goods, services, or organizations with which you may not agree.

Why the Scope Matters

Branding has a long and legitimate history not only in marketing but in other endeavors. (Attributions of paintings to "School of Rubens" show that brands have been important for almost half a millennium.)

An organization's Web site is part of its brand, along with marketing, logos, and other activities. The brand serves to identify and promote the organization; the Web site is just part of this work in support of the organization. However, there is another aspect of branding, and it works in reverse. The brand establishes authenticity and lends credence to the Web site.

This is the sense in which www.microsoft.com is Microsoft's Web site and www.w3c.org is the site of the World Wide Web Consortium. In each case, the site would not have its authority without the ownership; the organizations, too, would have decidedly different images if they did not have Web sites.

There is a direct relationship between a branded Web site and an enterprise's identity. If the enterprise has multiple brands, it may have multiple sites, with each one tied to a specific brand. (The example given previously of the Morgan Kaufmann Web site is one such case; the overall enterprise is Harcourt, yet Morgan Kaufmann Publishers is a recognized—and promoted—brand within the enterprise.)

Designing Your Site

People do not look at Web sites: they look at individual Web pages. The integration of those pages into a site may be clear in your mind, but it is not necessarily clear to users. In fact, the user with several windows open at a time may glance casually at the screen and mentally assemble the various pages into combinations that are irrelevant to the sites on which they are located. (Web sites that are defined by their connectivity characteristics—such as sites on an intranet—have different concerns. The following section deals with those.)

The scope of your site refers to its subject matter(s) and to the data that it contains. Whether the site presents a logical and coherent whole is a reflection on the clarity of its scope as well as its physical design. The physical design is implemented not only in the type of site that is created but also in the site-wide standards for page parts.

Types of Site Designs	Three basic types of page layout can define your site: unified, distributed, and fragmented. In addition to providing visual cues that the various pages are part of a single site, these layouts help people navigate through the entire site.
Unified	Unified sites have very strict design standards for pages: one layout is used for all pages (although sometimes two or more layouts are used for different types of pages). Limited modifications to these design standards are allowed, and they should be spelled out clearly. For example, the location, typefaces, and sizes of page titles and headings may be immutable, but the background color of the pages may be varied.

A unified site contains a guide to the entire site on each page. This may be a navigation panel with links to the major site pages, or it may be a much simpler set of links with links only to a home page (but to the same home page on each individual page).

Unified sites are easy to put up initially: you design one page, copy it, and then change the substance of each page. These sites tend to be difficult to maintain because any change to the site's general layout needs to be reflected on each page.

Unified sites are appropriate for small sites; they also can be maintained efficiently if the navigation aids are in a separate frame.

Distributed Distributed sites have design standards that are implemented on each page; however, somewhat greater leeway is allowed than with unified sites. Still, the combination of general layout, typeface, color, and other design characteristics presents a recognizable page for the site in question.

Distributed sites often have two-part navigation aids. One section provides links to the key areas of the site. In addition, a second set of links appears within each subsite site. Figure 7-1 shows several layouts for navigation aids in distributed sites.

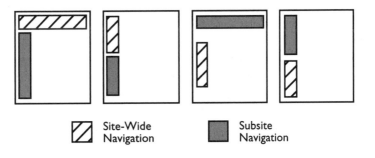

Site-Wide Navigation   Subsite Navigation

FIGURE 7-1. Layouts for Navigation Aids

The use of frames can make this implementation very easy. Even without frames, it is not particularly difficult. What is important is that the general layout of each page remains constant. If you change the relative locations of the site-wide and subsite navigation aids, you lose the consistency of the site.

In laying out a distributed site, remember to plan for maintenance. Deciding what links should be in the site-wide navigation aids needs to take into account the degree to which they may change, since a change may require a change to all pages on the site.

Fragmented

Fragmented sites have pages on them that have no design relationships with one another. At first, this may seem inadvisable; however, in some cases it is necessary.

If your Web site brings together pages generated by databases and application servers, your control over their layout may be constrained. Again, frames can sometimes help you out, but the preprogrammed pages may be so big that there is no reasonable room for your frames.

In general, you do not start out to have a fragmented Web site. You start out recognizing that certain pages—or groups of pages—will not be under your control and for that reason you have no choice but to have a fragmented Web site.

You can minimize the appearance of fragmentation by looking carefully at the design elements that you can control and using ones that will at least reflect the graphics, typefaces, colors, and layouts of your main site.

Web Page Parts

The parts of a Web page can be used to help in the design of the Web site. Table 7-2 lists each of the parts described in the previous chapter and how they can contribute to a unified Web site. (Remember that subsites can also be defined in this way; you may want to create a theme and variation for your site and its subsites; keeping some design elements constant and varying others will identify both the site itself and the subsites.)

Page Part	Role in a Web Site
Title	Make titles consistent. The site name may appear in each title.
Site Identifier	Should be in the same place and of the same size on each page on which it appears. (You may limit its appearance to certain types of pages.)
References	Site-wide references belong on home pages and home pages for subsites. References for individual pages may also include references to the site's home page (particularly if the site is large).
Ads	This is generally a site-wide decision.
Heading	Headings should be of the same size and location on all pages of the site. Fonts and colors may vary.
Site Navigation Aids	These should be in the same place on all pages on which they appear (they need not appear on all pages). If they do not appear on all pages, make it consistent which pages they do appear on.
Content	Site content should be consistent with regard to style. If you have a style guide for the site's enterprise, use it for the site. Check spelling and choose among alternatives on a site-wide basis.

TABLE 7-2. Parts for Interactive Pages

Page Part	Role in a Web Site
Action Buttons	These vary by page, but there should be site-wide standards for their size. If you use standard browser buttons on some pages, do not use customized "hot" GIFs on other pages. Make sure the user knows what can be clicked on.
Contact Information	Develop site-wide contact standards with regard to whether or not phone numbers and physical addresses are included. Also, consider whether contacts should be personal or by title. (That is, should the link be to "Art Director" or to "Terry Andrews"?)
Copyright Information	This can appear on each page or you can place a site-wide link to a single copyright page. Be consistent.
Creation and Modification Dates	Create a site-wide standard as to whether these appear or are only in (invisible) comments.
Author and Owner	Page ownership is managed in a top-down manner on the site. See "Assigning Responsibility" starting on page 236.
Counters and Logs	Before you go crazy with counters and logs, review what needs to be counted and logged. Site-wide standards (and site-wide counters) can help; avoid having separate types of visible counters on each page.

TABLE 7-2. Parts for Interactive Pages (Continued)

Structure of Web Sites

There are three aspects to Web site structure:

1. The domain name associated with the site

2. The physical location of the site

3. Web page characteristics

Domains and Domain Names

The first step in structuring your site is to give it a domain name and make certain that it is a name you can keep. It may seem obvious that you want it to be yourbusiness.com, but that name may not be available. You need to contact an Internet name registrar to find a name that is not reserved and then to reserve it.

The Accredited Registrar Directory is available on the Web at the following URL—http://www.internic.net/regist.html. Any of the registrars listed can help you locate and reserve a name. Their Web sites let you do this online. Note that if you have not yet settled on a physical location for your Web site, you may have to pay simply to reserve a name. If you have settled on a physical location, your ISP can do the registration for you—but be certain to check if there is an added cost. The only information that you need is the name of the Web server and the IP address of the Web server; your ISP should supply you with both of these. Have them ready before registering your site.

The issues involved in scoping a site ("Scoping a Web Site" starting on page 154) and in taking control of a Web project that may be teetering on the brink of disarray ("Taking Control of a Web-Based Enterprise" starting on page 14) come into play here. You need to identify your site appropriately so that people—both users and your colleagues—know what it contains.

Protecting Your Domain's Scope

You need to guard against two types of ambiguity, just as you do with scoping. If you "temporarily" park your Web site on someone else's site (or on a free section of another site), you will wind up with a confused domain. It may make sense to you that your domain name is www.commercialservicepro-vider.com/users/~yourbusiness/index.html, but that does not fit easily on a business card. Likewise, you have to guard against farming out sections of your site to others: it confuses your (and their) message.

Your domain name is the name that you will promote: in advertisements, on business cards, in e-mail signatures, and so forth. Make certain that it is a name that will not change. That means enforcing fairly high-level addressing. If your customer service area can be found at www.yourcompany.com/customerservice/index.html, consider whether or not it is better to direct people simply to www.yourcompany.com and have navigation aids to take them from there. That way if your customer service area changes to a customer support division, you do not have to redo links.

Redirection

One method that you can use to keep your site in order is redirection. With this technique, when a user goes to a page, that page automatically diverts the user to another location. You see this frequently when you encounter a page that says, "This page has moved."

Using redirection as standard navigation is not a good idea: it means that the server (and the user's browser) must process two pages rather than one. However, if you are confronted with a situation in which a URL you have distributed must be changed, it may be the only way to deal with it.

Redirection is managed with a meta-tag in the header section of an HTML document. (It can also be accomplished with a script—that occurs in cases where the redirection may vary depending on which browser the person is using, what type of computer is requesting the page, and so forth. A script can redirect based on any of these choices.)

The following HTML code shows a simple redirection page:

```
<HTML>
<!DOCTYPE HTML PUBLIC "-//W3C//DTD HTML 3.2 Final//EN">
<HEAD>
    <TITLE>Sample Redirection Page</TITLE>
    <META HTTP-EQUIV="Refresh"
        CONTENT="5; URL=www.yourdomain.com/pageaddress.html">
</HEAD>
<BODY>
    This page has moved to
    <A HREF="http://www.yourdomain.com/pageaddress.html">
    http://www.yourdomain.com/pageaddress.html</A>
</BODY>
</HTML>
```

You can copy this code exactly, making changes to the underlined segments:

- Insert a title for the page that is appropriate.

- Inside the Refresh meta-tag, insert the number of seconds that you want the browser to wait before transferring the user. In this case, the value is 5 seconds. (This is the first double-underlined code.)

- Also inside the Refresh meta-tag, insert the URL of the page to which the user should be redirected. (This is the second double-underlined code.)

- In the anchor element (<A>), place the URL of the page to which the user should go.

- Also in the anchor element, place the URL a second time. This will display the URL and make it a link for the user to click on.

The double-underlined code is all that is required. The title code is good Web manners, and the use of the anchor element allows browsers that do not support the Refresh meta-tag to display a link for people to click. Most browsers do support the Refresh meta-tag, so you can often omit this.

Physical Locations

You need a place for your site. If you already have an ISP, you probably will start there. However, you can mix and match physical locations within a domain name.

Your domain name must be directed to a specific ISP; that ISP must be the same one that manages your e-mail. (Note that it does not have to be the ISP where you actually get your mail, but it must be able to forward your mail appropriately.)

Links on your pages can send users to various places—on a variety of servers. Note, however, that if you are releasing the URLs of individual pages, it is confusing to people to find them on a variety of servers. If you direct people to your home page, you can keep the distributed locations from confusing people.

The physical connection that you make to the Internet will allow you to connect to other Internet locations. Thus, if your Web server is located thousands of miles away, you need only connect to a nearby Internet service provider and then use FTP to get to your Web site to update pages. This is discussed at length in Chapter 6, "Choosing Your Internet Service Provider," in *Database-Driven Web Sites*.

Web Page Characteristics

You can use the characteristics of Web pages as described in the previous chapter to define your site. (If you do not do this in an organized way, your site will be defined by the chance combinations of characteristics that your pages display.)

Table 7-3 lists the characteristics and the roles that they can play in your Web site.

Characteristics	Role in a Web Site
Languages	Decide on a site-wide structure. Will there be separate subsites for different languages? Will you use full translations or have a primary language for the entire site and index information in other languages?
Images	Set a limited number of image options. Will images be inline or presented as links to graphics files? Will they appear in specific places on pages?
Page Size	Set a preferred page size and stick to it for the site. If pages need to be larger or smaller, open them in other windows. Avoid minor variations in page size that require users to resize their browser windows constantly.
Bandwidth	For high-speed intranets and other environments without bandwidth concerns, make it clear that people should not waste time economizing on transmission time.
Style Sheets	If you use style sheets, use them consistently across the site.
Cookies	If you use cookies, make certain that your site's privacy policy mentions them and that any page using a cookie links to (or contains) your privacy policy.
Scripting Languages	Select your scripting language and stick to it to avoid maintenance nightmares.
Programming Languages	Same as for scripting languages.

TABLE 7-3. Characteristics for Structuring a Web Site

Characteristics	Role in a Web Site
Downloading Files	If you have many downloads (such as promotional material or manuals), consider setting up a separate server for downloading so that these files are not scattered about your site. The performance of a server for downloads is different from one serving up Web pages.
Ratings	If your site uses any ratings, decide what they will be. Since filters often screen out unrated pages, make certain that all pages are rated.
Obligatory Hardware and Software	Make clear to your staff and your users what is required and then move on.
Recommended Hardware and Software	Minimize features that may or may not work (or that work differently in various configurations). But make it clear what the configurations you support are.
Composite Pages (Frames)	This is a site-wide choice. If you use frames, make certain that links open consistently in the right frame or a new window. The TARGET attribute must be set in all links on a frame-aware site—even for pages that do not employ frames.
Caching Information	Speed up your site's performance by including caching information. This may require structuring the physical location of files so that certain directories with specific caching parameters contain otherwise unrelated files.

TABLE 7-3. Characteristics for Structuring a Web Site (Continued)

Characteristics	Role in a Web Site
Security	Decide what parts of your site are secure. Do not do this randomly. You need to implement security coherently across the site.
Privacy	Make certain that your site's privacy policy is contained on or linked to every page. Make certain that everyone is aware of the policy so that they do not accidentally violate it by collecting and misusing information.
Site Awareness	For even the largest sites, there are probably a half dozen to a dozen locations that should appear as links on almost all pages. This is site awareness, and it should be consistent. Make certain that these links will not change.
Content	Just as for printed material, you need a style sheet for content. Is it to be formal? Friendly?

TABLE 7-3. Characteristics for Structuring a Web Site (Continued)

Summary

This chapter has provided a way of talking about your site itself; together with the previous chapter in which characteristics of individual pages were identified, it provides the framework for discussing the site's structure and functionality without recourse to vague and imprecise feelings.

The next step is to move on to the specific needs of different types of sites: informational, interactive, and transactional sites.

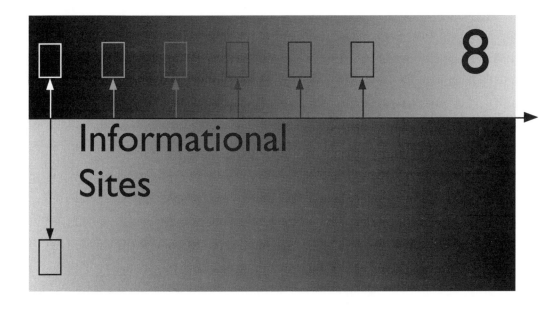

8

Informational Sites

This chapter deals with the presentation of information on Web sites (including individual pages, subsites, and entire sites). The focus is not on graphical design elements but rather on the way the site works. The flow of data on informational sites and pages is from the site to the user.

First, the most fundamental issue of informational sites is explored: are you presenting information or are you allowing people to look at information? In other words, "Who's in Charge?" (or in still other terms, is the information pulled or pushed to the user?).

Once you have decided who's in charge, the remaining sections of the chapter help you implement your policies and your site. You need to describe the information in such a way that people can use it as they (and you) see fit. Issues relating to the presentation of information include links, downloadable files, and Web pages themselves.

Organizing the information is important not just to your users but also to the performance of your entire site. If the chunks of information are too big, your users may go away in disgust—and your server may bog down fulfilling requests in too much detail.

As always on the Web, security is a major concern (and one that is frequently overlooked). Frequently your information is your most valuable asset; you need to protect it from theft and from unauthorized use.

Finally, the logical design of informational sites is presented, along with the archetypical pages. It is possible to put up a large number of Web pages on one or more sites without considering these issues. However, considering them will make the difference between a site that "just grew" and one that makes sense and provides benefits to users and owners alike.

Note in this chapter that "site" is used in all of its senses—from an individual page, to a portion of a large site, or a site itself.

Who's in Charge?

This may be the most frequently overlooked aspect of planning an informational site. All too often, people just "put up a Web page." Users complain that they cannot find information—and the Web site designer or owner points out that the information is indeed on the site. End of discussion, in most cases. But that is not a satisfactory resolution.

The User

In many cases, it is the user who should be in charge of the site's information. That is, the information should be made available so that the user has a very high probability of locating what is needed.

It is obvious that the user should be in charge in any site that promotes or sells things. Making things hard to find is not good marketing.

Who Are the Users?

If you have decided that the user is in charge, you need to identify who the user is—or, more often, who they are. Sometimes, this is simple. A financial services company's internal Web site may be open only to its employees—and then only to those employees who deal with customer service. You know who your users are—right down to their names.

On the other hand, an e-commerce store may have a variety of users—browsers, shoppers, frequent shoppers, and so forth. Each group may need different ways of navigating the site.

Consider, too, your users' frame of mind. This is scarcely trivial. If your site provides a help desk's information, your users may be frustrated—even angry. Cuteness will probably not be appreciated.

While respecting privacy, you can often gather and maintain information about your users to pierce the veil of anonymity people think the Web provides. Refer to "Privacy" starting on page 59 and "Gatekeepers" starting on page 183 later in this chapter for more information.

Qualifying Users

Sales and marketing people use the word "qualify" to describe the process by which they determine whether an individual really is capable of purchasing a large diamond ring or palatial home or is "just shopping." You may be able to clearly identify qualified users—or perhaps just disqualified users. In any case, the more information you have about who you want to use your site and who you do not want to use the site, the better you will be able to implement a successful informational site.

Do not be swept away by the lure of the large numbers of people on the Internet. More is almost always not better. A site that provides excellent service to 5 people is better than one that fails to provide service to 10,000.

The Site Owner

In some cases, publication on the Web (like publication in the legal notices at the back of some newspapers) is a requirement that needs to be honored—but no more than that. If someone finds the information they are looking for, that is all well and good. But it does not matter to the site owner.

In a very few cases, publication on the Web is designed to fulfill some type of requirement, and that publication is deliberately made obscure. (This is scarcely limited to the Web—previews of movies are often held in out-of-the-way places so that producers and directors can get a sense of how audiences may respond.)

One major software company is notorious for hiding information on its site. In litigation (of which it has been involved in a lot), they have repeatedly testified to adhering to the letter of agreements—publication—without paying attention to the spirit of the agreements—promotion of the information.

You cannot proceed to address the issues that follow in this chapter until you determine whether your site's goal is to publish the information you want to publish or to provide the information your users want.

Describing the Information

Once you have decided who's in charge, you need to describe the information on the site appropriately. If you are providing information to users so that they can be in charge, this means clarifying what you have in terms that they can understand and in ways that make sense to them. If you are in charge, you still need to describe the information, albeit in terms that make sense to you.

This section omits the situation cited previously in which you are deliberately not interested in making information accessible although you have posted it to your Web site.

What is the Information?

Once again, the most basic question you need to answer is omitted in many cases: just what is the information that you are presenting? At the level of a subsite or Web page, this is the same issue as scoping a site, discussed in the previous chapter.

Titles and Terminology

Take advantage of—and beware of—terminology that verges on jargon. This is the simplest way to qualify your users or to open the site to the world. Every Web (or library) user has endless examples of information that is hidden in plain sight through the use of arcane terminology in its title.

In particular, be sensitive to the nonlinear nature of the Web. If you use search engines, you frequently come across pages with titles such as, "Another Example." Of what? The search engine has found the word or phrase for which you have searched, but you may not have a clue why it is relevant.

Presenting the Information

There are four basic ways of presenting information on a Web page:

1. Inline information is information—text or graphics—that appears on the page itself.

2. Linked information is information presented on another page, accessed via a hyperlink. Internal links are to pages that you control.

3. External links are to pages that are controlled by others.

4. Information can also be presented in other types of files. Typically, these are either downloaded to the user's disk or opened by helper applications in the user's browser.

Inline
Information

Inline information is the simplest way of presenting information on the Web. It can consist of text or graphics; it can be complex in its layout and structure, or it can be ordinary, unstyled text.

The simplest page with inline information contains one word: Hello. Here is the HTML code for that page:

```
<HTML>
<HEAD>
</HEAD>
<P>Hello</P>
</BODY>
</HTML>
```

The examples in this section are not designed to make you a Web designer; rather they are designed to help you find your way around Web pages that you may be reviewing. In a pinch, you can use them as primitive templates.

Replace the underlined code with whatever text you want and you will have your own Web page. (The underlining is for illustration only; do not use it on your Web page.)

As with everything on a Web site, there are rarely hard and fast rules on when to use what. Here are the pros and cons of using inline information.

First the pros:

- These are the simplest pages to create.

- Particularly for inexperienced Web users, these are the simplest pages to view.

- All the information is in one place. This makes managing maintenance easier.

- It is easy to print a single Web page (even if it takes several printed pages).

Here are some of the disadvantages:

- These pages can be quite lengthy. Download time can be unacceptable.

- Furthermore, if users typically want only a small portion of the page's information, the download time can be disproportionate to the benefit of the information.

- Finding wanted information on a lengthy page can be difficult.

Linked Information: Internal

You can split the information onto several pages, providing links to get to the next information. Here is the simplest code for a link to internal information. The page displays the text Past Graduates as a link (colored and underlined in most browsers). If you click on it, the page alumni.html is opened in the same window, replacing the page you are viewing.

```
<HTML>
<HEAD>
</HEAD>
<P><A HREF="alumni.html">Past Graduates</A></P>
</BODY>
</HTML>
```

Replace the underlined code as appropriate for your purpose. Past Graduates is what appears on the page; alumni.html is the address of the page to go to.

Again, there are pros and cons. Here are some of the advantages of using internal links:

- Download time is usually shorter because the information is split up.

- Finding relevant information from within a large corpus of information is easier for users. This is particularly important if users typically want only a small amount of the data.

- Maintenance can be easier, since only portions of the information need to be modified.

Among the disadvantages are these:

- It is harder to print the information; multiple pages have to be viewed and printed.

- It is hard for users to pass along the information; what is a single body of information to them may be a collection of URLs that another person would not traverse or would traverse differently.

Linked Information: External

You can incorporate links to external Web sites and pages. All of the issues (positive and negative) of internal links apply. There are two additional points to consider.

In coding an external link, the complete URL needs to be given. Thus, the code in the preceding example would need to be changed as follows:

```
<P><A HREF="http://www.sitename.com/alumni.html">Past Gradu-
ates</A></P>
```

The boldface text is added so that the complete URL is given; the page alumni.html is located on another site (www.sitename.com).

You can use this notation even on your own site. However, providing the full URL as shown here can complicate your life in moving files around on your own site;.

In addition to the pros and cons of internal links, two big ones must be added:

- By incorporating data from other sites onto your own, you can provide resources far beyond your own. This is the point of the World Wide Web.

- By using resources that you do not control, your links can break without your knowing it.

In order to minimize such broken links, you can use some or all of these techniques:

- Link to the highest reasonable page on the external site. (In other words, www.ibm.com is likely to be around; www.ibm.com/northamerica/testsite/java-beans/trialballoon.html may not be long lived.) However, make certain that your link makes sense to your user. ("Why am I suddenly on IBM's site?") The practice of linking to internal pages is known as **deep linking**.

- Periodically run a utility to check for broken links on your site. Your ISP can recommend such a product; many ISPs provide such services on their own.

- When linking to external sites, give preference to those that you know best. (This, too, is common sense; unfortunately, it bears repeating. There are Web pages with links that their authors have never even seen, much less tested.)

Downloadable Information

Finally, you can present information as downloadable files. There are several reasons to do this:

- If you want the data to be interpreted by a program other than a browser, this is the best (and usually only) choice. An example is a spreadsheet that should be seen in a spreadsheet program like Excel, a movie, or a document that needs to appear in its printed format.

- This can be a more efficient way to download large amounts of data and lengthy documents. Formats other than HTML can be very efficient.

- Certain types of information really benefit from appearing in page images. For example, if you are posting a form to be used by employees in applying for vacation, the printed version of a downloaded form should be as indistinguishable as possible from the version that an employees gets at the office. Likewise, documents that are to be discussed at a meeting benefit from appearing consistent: the sentence at the top of page three is the same sentence for all people. (This is not true for HTML pages, where pagination is a function of printing, font size, and so forth.)

Portable Document Format

One of the most widely used downloadable formats is PDF—Adobe's Portable Document Format. This is a simple format that is based on PostScript, the encoding used for most printing on personal computers. There are three software components to the PDF system, and there are three steps to take to create a PDF document.

The software involved in PDF consists of three products:

1. Acrobat Reader is available free from www.adobe.com. It is included as a plug-in or helper application with many browsers. Many users have Acrobat Reader already. It is used to display PDF files either in a browser or as a stand-alone application on the user's personal computer.

2. Adobe Acrobat is a commercially available product that provides additional functionality beyond that of Acrobat Reader. This additional functionality includes the ability to annotate documents. It is not necessary to view documents.

3. Acrobat Distiller is the product that produces PDF files. It is incorporated into some other products; its functionality is part of Mac OS X, in which PDF is a native document type. (That means that you can save a document in Mac OS X as a PDF document without going through any additional steps.) Acrobat Distiller—or a functional equivalent—is required for you to produce PDF files. It is not needed for viewing.

The three steps to producing PDF files are these:

1. With the document open, choose Print as you normally would do. Select the option, Print to File, and name the resulting file in any way that you want.

2. Run Acrobat Distiller, and open the file created in step 1. (It will likely have a suffix .ps for PostScript.) A new file will be created with the suffix .pdf.

3. Upload the pdf file to your Web site and create a link to it from your page. Such a link might look like this:

```
<P><A HREF="telephonebook.pdf">Directory (PDF)</A></P>
```

Note that individual pages of a site can be made downloadable. There are some people who want to "download a site"—possibly because they feel more comfortable with hard copy. A site that is designed for downloading eschews links and other aspects of the Web. It is normally a failure. Download pages, not sites.

Organizing the Information

If you split up the information on a page, you need to decide how to do so. When moving information from another medium (such as print), there is a temptation to make each printed page a single Web page. This is normally quite wasteful.

Splitting up the information in a logical manner—with each page of a different length—is very Web-like; users appreciate it. Avoid artificial breaks in the material.

You need to decide how to let users navigate through the material. Links (internal and external) let them jump around. For sequential material, it is common to provide the following buttons at the bottom (and top) of a page:

```
Previous - Next
   Contents
```

This lets you go to the next or previous page as well as to a contents page. It also traps you.

Far better is a navigation structure such as this:

<u>Previous</u> <u>1</u> <u>2</u> <u>3</u> <u>4</u> <u>5</u> <u>Next</u>
<u>Contents</u>

Users can move forward or back with Next and Previous; but they can also skip around within the pages that they have viewed or might view.

Remember that the page numbers are for the user's convenience. They can link to pages anywhere on your site. However, if you are using a numbering scheme like this, make certain that the highlighted number on page 3 matches the user's expectation. You need to implement this numbering scheme at the bottom (and top) of each page in the sequence.

Protecting the Information

As always on the Web, you need to consider protection of your information. Two points should be addressed: gatekeepers and security.

Gatekeepers

Before allowing users to view your information, you may require them to log in. This may involve actually paying for information; it may also be as simple as simply providing their name and e-mail address. Gatekeepers drastically reduce traffic to a page. In many cases, that is desirable (this is all part of qualifying users of your site).

Implementing Gatekeepers

There are two basic ways to implement gatekeepers:

1. **Directory Access on the HTTP Server.** You can place the page(s) in a directory protected with access controls (realms in Apache terms). To do this, you need to create a directory that requires users to log in the first

time they request a file that is in that directory. This requires the assistance of your ISP or network coordinator in setting up the directory. However, once it is set up, they no longer need to be involved.

The advantage is that you can use a single directory for many protected pages. You can also easily implement shared userids—useful for granting access to a large group of individuals (your company's sales staff, for example). Once the directory has been accessed during a browser's session, it is unlocked and registration is not required for any of the pages within that directory.

2. **Cookies**. You can implement a cookie on the page(s) to be protected. If the cookie is not found, you request the information and store the cookie; if it is, you display the data. This does not require the assistance of your ISP or network coordinator, but it does require you to implement cookies with JavaScript or another programming language. (Most Web development applications implement cookies for you.)

    This method lends itself well to large numbers of userids that are created on the fly by individuals. By modifying the expiration date, you can leave cookies around for a given period of time (days or months), for the user's session, or only for a moment or two. This helps you implement security in which you require re-registration after a period of time.

Security

If your information needs to be secure, you need to take steps such as those described in *Database-Driven Web Sites* and *Application Servers: Powering the Web-Based Enterprise*. Start from the assumption that everything you post to the Web needs to be made secure. This assumption—that a lack of security is the exception rather than that security is the exception—will save you from grief.

Even on an intranet, the ease of moving digital information can let your Web pages and their information travel within your organization in ways you do not anticipate—or want.

Designing the Site

The information you present may be inline, provided with internal or external links, or downloaded. In addition to the information, there are five common types of pages on an informational site (or subsite).

Home Page

This page contains basic information about the site—its purpose, its owner, and how to use it. It may also contain warnings (in the case of complex or inappropriate material). For small sites (or subsites), this page presents the information; no additional pages are required.

Gatekeepers

If the site is protected with a gatekeeper,[1] it can be placed in front of, on, or behind the home page.

In Front of the Home Page   When in front of the home page, it means that users can see nothing about your page without logging in (or paying a fee).

---

1. For more information, see Chapter 15, "Security," in *Database-Driven Web Sites*. It includes examples of code for using cookies, which can be used to implement gatekeeping functions.

On the Home Page   In this case, the home page is itself a gatekeeper. You ask people to log on (and/or pay); however, information about your site is available on the page.

Behind the Home Page   When a gatekeeper is placed behind the home page, users can see what might be inside by reading the home page; they must register (and/or pay) to see individual pages. Placing gatekeepers behind the home page has two benefits:

1.   Some pages can be gated; others can be public.

2.   If users bypass your home page, it is easy to catch them with individual page gatekeepers.

Bypassing the Home Page

A common failing of Web site design is to think that your users will see your home page and proceed in an orderly fashion (*your* orderly fashion) through the site. People bookmark useful pages and jump around—that is the nature of the Web.

A home page replete with your organization's mission statement, photos of the founders, and tributes from clients or stockholders may make a wonderful presentation to friends, relatives, or colleagues, but it is usually a big bore—particularly the fiftieth time it is seen.

For people to see your home page, it must be useful—even essential. Here are some ways to make your home page productive:

- **Make it essential**. If you place a gatekeeper or logon entry on the home page, users cannot proceed without starting there. (Remember, though, that this will reduce traffic to your internal pages. Consider your site's goal.)

- **Keep it simple**. Remove the photos of your founder's pet goldfish that died last year. Remove the mission statement and the charter. Place them on other pages.

- **Keep its structure constant**. If your users visit the site frequently, they will not want to have to read the entire page to find out how to get to the same information they got to last week.

- **Keep the information fresh**. Within the constant structure, keep appropriate information up to date. One way of doing this is to place commercial services such as the weather or stock quotes on your home page. Do not place links—people will just wander off; rather use one of the products that lets you place the data on your page. Of course, the information needs to be relevant.

- **Make it load fast**. Use every trick in the book to make this the highest performance page on your site. Caching and frames can be used to improve performance. On intranets or if your site is used frequently by devoted users, try to make it the start-up site for your user's browser so that it will be loaded when the browser has finished starting up. Even better, make the browser an application that launches automatically at start-up. When the user turns on the computer, the browser will launch and the site will be loaded. (That is not only efficient and fast, but it is also annoying if your site is not that important to your users. Be careful.)

Site Map	This provides an overall view of the site—usually in graphic terms. If the site is at all complex, this can be very helpful to users. However, if the site frequently changes, this site map can become quite useless if it becomes out of date.

One way of preventing this problem is for the site map to point to general (unchanging) areas of the site rather than to individual pages.

The site map may be a link on all pages on the site. It is irrelevant for small sites. Get ideas by exploring sites on the Internet and seeing which ones seem easy to use.

Retrieval Page

This page provides the ability to find information on the site. It may let people search the site for words or phrases. This can be confined to page titles or to the full contents of pages. In simpler cases, the retrieval page can be a set of links to other pages on your site with no searching allowed.

The retrieval page and its features may be a link on all pages of the site. Alternatively, it can be an element (or frame) on each page.

Site search is useful when people do not know what information is available. When they do know what they are searching for, the site map or even direct links from the home page are preferable.

Site search can be implemented with a separate page or with a search section on all (or selected) pages. There are many site search tools available. You can license heavy-duty search engines from the major searching companies if your site is big; for smaller sites, shareware Perl scripts may do the trick.

Search or Link Results

When someone has clicked a link or conducted a search, there are two possibilities:

1. A list of pages that may or may not contain the information can be displayed—a summary display page.

2. The information can be displayed in a full record display.

Summary Display Page

These pages are like the typical output from search engines—a list of pages that satisfy the search. Each entry has a link so that you can click it to go to the referenced page. Often summary display pages contain additional information about the referenced page—such as when it was last updated. You can frequently sort and resort the summaries to view the information in various ways. There may be multiple pages, each one displaying a certain number of references.

Observe your own Web surfing and get to know your site's data to determine what to include in lists of intermediate results. One very efficient way of setting up a site is so that the list of possible information resources often contains the information itself. Thus, if you have pages for individual employees, it might be useful to establish the convention that each page title includes the employee's phone extension and mail stop. For more detailed information, users need to go to the individual pages; however, for the most frequently requested information, the summary data is sufficient.

Full Record Display

This is the display of the data itself. Remember that users do not want to use search engines—they want the information. Check how many mouse clicks it takes to get to your full record displays.

Evaluating Your Site

Subject to privacy constraints, you can monitor how people use your retrieval pages. This can be an invaluable tool in developing and improving your site.

Your privacy policy should make it clear how you are using information. The critical issue in most cases is whether you associate any identifying information with the traffic patterns on your site. In other words, if you check to see what people are searching for and what pages they visit, that is very different from associating e-mail addresses or other identifying information with those searches.

| What Do People Look For? | You have an irrefutable list of what some people want to see. If you repeatedly get visitors to your site who are looking for information you do not have, you can either place it on your site, place links to locations where the information can be found, or you can change your site's name or other identifying information so that these people do not waste their time and your bandwidth. |

| What Searches Fail? | You have a good indication of where your site is in trouble. Look for requests for information that is already on the site. Do not dismiss them because the user does not know how to navigate: make your navigation more intuitive. |

| Estimating Off-Site Behavior | If you monitor the site closely, you may be able to establish a ratio between overall visitors and those who post queries. You also may be able to establish ratios between queries and other behavior—such as purchases of items. |

Summary

Informational sites—the original type of sites on the Web—present information in formats and combinations selected dynamically by users. This dynamic selection can involve sophisticated searches or the very basic selection process of simply clicking on a link.

The next chapter moves on to the more complex world of interactive sites in which the user's input is captured and processed.

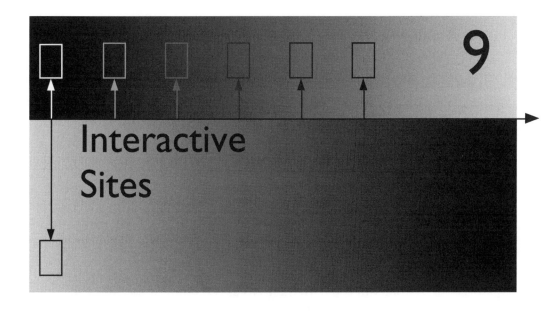

9

Interactive Sites

Interactive sites collect information from users and display it on their pages. Examples of interactive sites and pages are calendars and time schedules that can be updated by the public, community discussion groups (for any sort of community), as well as job and for sale listings. Interactive pages also include a wide variety of feedback forms, e-mail templates, and other devices that provide input to the site owner and not to other users.

Many of the issues discussed in the previous chapter still apply; these include describing the information, presenting the information, and organizing the information. However, interactive sites and pages have their own considerations when it comes to who is in charge, protecting the information, and site designs. They are addressed in this chapter.

(Note that transactions—extended interactions involving the exchange of value—are covered in the next chapter.)

Interactive Sites: Letting Users Update Your Site

Interactive pages involve a data flow to the site. Interactive sites (or subsites) present user-entered data. This may be done to share data in a community or workgroup (a calendar, for example); it may also be done to provide a changing and interesting set of information to users. Once you have set up your infrastructure, updates are easily made.

Sometimes the interactivity is the point of the site. That is the case with a community calendar or other shared data. Other times, the interactivity is a sideline: for example, letting sales representatives rotate in posting specific items to your home page allows for "bargains of the day," but the bulk of your site will not change from day to day.

There is a general feeling that limited frequent updates draw people to a site—that is, if they are interested in the information. Items such as "Joke of the Day" and a local weather forecast may fall into this category. But if the jokes are poor and the weather forecasts for somewhere far away, it may all be for naught. As always, consider what your users want, not what you want to provide.

Who's in Charge?

In the previous chapter, it was sufficient to consider whether users or site owners are in charge. With interactive sites, there are two types of users—the inquiring user and the participating user.

The Inquiring User

The inquiring user is the same user described in the previous chapter.

The Participating User

Here you have a major set of issues to decide about. Interactive sites can be updated by internal users—your employees, for example; they can also be updated by external users—anyone with access to a Web browser. Your site's purpose should help you determine which of these groups should be allowed to update the site.

An interactive site is a good way to spread the burden of updating a site throughout an organization. Rather than funneling all calendar entries to the Web team, you can let people enter their own data. You can create separate data flows for internal and external entries, as you will see later in this chapter.

The Site Owner

You also need to decide what degree of control you want to exercise over the content that is posted by people to your site. Are you hosting an open forum in which anyone can participate on any subject? Or are you claiming some direct or indirect authorization for the site's content?

Many people have a reluctance to open their site to public input; this is based on many cases in which open forums have been hijacked by off-topic (or at least unpleasant) postings. However, you can manage these problems if you look at the techniques later in this chapter (see "Protecting the Information" starting on page 201 and "Review Page (Optional)" starting on page 203).

One of the chief benefits of an open forum is that it can provide your site with a range of changing information that you could not provide by yourself.

Organizing the Information

Interactive sites are usually highly structured. Data will be flowing from users onto your site, and you need to have places to put it. When you design a Web page, you can place text and graphics where you choose; to support interactivity, you need slots into which user input will automatically be placed. Otherwise, you need to allow users to create and upload HTML—and that is rarely desirable.

Note that this may feel like a backward approach to the problem. When designing a Web page, many people start with the information; they then organize it, categorize it, and finally make it look coherent. When you do not know what the content will be (since it will be provided interactively by users), you must start with the organization and categorization, supply the layout, and then trust that the incoming data will fit.

You can use e-mail or HTML forms to collect the data and send it to your site. For more information on processing the information, see "Sending Information to a Server" starting on page 97.

Categorizing the Data

This actually can be a very efficient way of working. Instead of an ex post facto categorizing, users must categorize their input in advance. (This also sometimes has the added benefit of clarifying users' thoughts.) For example, an interactive site for a community group may allow users to post messages and information in categories such as traffic, economic development, sustainable growth, or technology. If there is no Other category, posters will need to make a choice from one of the categories you have provided.

Structuring the Data

Interactive sites almost always rely on a database for their data. This may be a high-end database such as DB2 or Oracle; it can also be a midrange product specifically designed for integration with the Web such as FileMaker Pro. It can even be a Perl file.

A mistake that most people make is in being stingy with database fields. They take up very little disk space, and a proliferation of database fields rarely affects performance seriously. You will note that most of this information is not displayed; it provides the infrastructure that helps you manage your site.

If you are not used to using a database, you may be surprised to learn that much of the processing you think you may have to do can be done in the database. Many people think that they retrieve data from a database—and then sort it, loop through the data selecting certain types of records, and so forth. Instead, you build all of these functions into your database query: you request that the data be returned sorted and that it include only the types of data that you want.

Table 9-1 shows the database fields that you should have in your supporting database.

Field	Description
Project	This field (which the user will likely not see) can let you use a single database for a number of projects. Use a hidden field on the HTML form to indicate that an entry is for joke of the day, calendar, suggestion, or other project. Whether you share a database among several projects or not depends on the traffic each project generates.
Title	Each item in the database should be named. You may generate these names automatically (either for the database or just for the Web site's display). Titles can help you create threads of messages. If you add a Reply button to a data display screen, you can use JavaScript to bring the title of the retrieved data forward automatically and insert it in the appropriate field of the new item. (Automatically generating the title, particularly in the case of replies, can make your database neater. People have an annoying tendency to start new threads, mistype references to previous titles, and otherwise litter the database.)
Summary	You may want a summary of each data element. This is particularly valuable if the data elements can be lengthy or if they can consist of graphics or other nontextual information without any textual equivalent. This field (if it is used) should be severely limited in length.
Category	This is the single category in which the data is primarily stored. Be careful about allowing an Other category: everything will wind up there.
Priority	You may want to order items on the page or select only certain types of items.
Security	You can set security levels for records so that, for instance, some are retrieved only when employees (rather than the public) visit the site.
Rating	Ratings can help select types of information based on any criteria that you set.

TABLE 9-1. Database Fields for an Interactive Database

Field	Description
Keywords	This field lets users (or an editor) specify a number of keywords to assist in searching. Note that keeping up keywords fields can be time consuming. With the speed of modern computers, it is almost always faster just to search the text of items for wanted words rather than to maintain a separate keyword field. For that reason, you may choose to omit this field.
URL	If a URL is associated with the item, you often want to display it as a link. You will need to repeat the field: in the first case, it serves as the destination for the HREF attribute (this is the actual link); in the second case, the text of the URL is displayed. The URL will appear only once on the Web page that is generated.

The code to do this in Microsoft Access and FileMaker is included here for reference.

<A HREF="<%URL%>"> <%URL%> </A>

<A HREF="[FMP-FIELD: URL]">[FMP-FIELD: URL] </A>

This might also be a case in which you want to bracket the code with if statements—if the URL is an optional field in the database. You might also want to add text such as "For further information see." Here is that full-blown example

<%if>
For further information see
<A HREF="<%URL%>"> <%URL%> </A>
<%endif%>

[FMP-IF: URL .neq.]
For further information see
<A HREF="[FMP-FIELD: URL]">[FMP-FIELD: URL] </A>
[/FMP-IF]

TABLE 9-1. Database Fields for an Interactive Database (Continued)

Field	Description

URL Name	Instead of displaying the URL for a link, you can create an anchor for the URL and display a name for the link (this is the difference between displaying http://www.ibm.com and IBM Corporation); the underlying link is the same. If you want to do this, add a field to the database for the URL name.
	
	The code to do this in Microsoft Access and FileMaker is included here for reference.
	
	`<A HREF="<%URL%>"> <%URLName%> </A>`
	
	`<A HREF="[FMP-FIELD: URL]"> [FMP-FIELD: URLName] </A>`

Information (Text)	This is the basic information to be shared.
Information (Image)	You may add an image field to most modern databases; it may be used to augment the textual information or to replace it.
Information (Blob)	Similarly, you can use a generalized field to store movies, animations, and other dynamic data.
Author ID	You usually need to keep track of the author of each item. This may be a collection of fields (including address, e-mail, and so forth), or it may be an ID that is expanded in a related file to the full information about an individual.
Posting Time Stamp	You should keep track of when each item is posted. This time stamp should be calculated automatically by the computer on which the database resides (not inserted into a data entry form by a browser); use the database's computer as the arbiter of time.
Revisor ID	If items are revised or edited, you may want to keep track of who did it.

TABLE 9-1. Database Fields for an Interactive Database (Continued)

Field	Description
Last Revision Time Stamp	In some high-security applications, you want to keep track of each revision; in most cases, however, it is sufficient to keep track of the date and time of initial entry and then of the date and time of the latest revision (if any).
Display Status	This field allows you to mark an item as being ready to display; a database query that generates a summary display should include only those items with a satisfactory display status. (This allows for editing and approval.)
Content Status	You may need a displayable field that describes some status of the data. In a calendar, this may be an indicator such as "Open to the Public." Different types of entries may have different types of statuses; having a separate field can make retrieval easier.
Starting Time Stamp	You can use this time stamp to control a range of dates and times during which the item is displayed. For databases containing calendars and schedules, this allows you to enter data in advance and specify its period of display without having to update the database at specific times.
Ending Time Stamp	Working with the starting time stamp, this field lets you terminate listings.

TABLE 9-1. Database Fields for an Interactive Database (Continued)

Protecting the Information

You need to protect the data not just in the same way you do informational data (that is, by controlling access) but also by taking steps to make certain that your Web site does not become an outlet for inappropriate material. A review process, as described later in this chapter, can help in this regard.

You can also take steps to avoid problems by clearly specifying on your input forms what types of material are inappropriate (pornography, copyrighted items, and so forth). In addition, you can recognize that certain types of input you solicit (such as a joke of the day) are likely to generate copyrighted materials that should not be posted.

Designing the Site

In addition to pages that you need to let users find the information on your site (as discussed in the previous chapter), there are several pages that you need specifically to support interactive sites.

Home Page

Your home page should indicate that this site is interactive. Those indications come in several areas:

- Your copyright notice must recognize that you are incorporating material from users. You need either to exclude interactive material or to recognize that you cannot know what will be on your site. Use phrases such as "All trademarks are the property of their owners" to encompass variable data.

- Your privacy notice should reflect that users can submit information which may be published. It is hard to imagine someone going to the trouble of composing a message to be posted to your site and then objecting to it, but stranger things have happened. Make it clear whether items will be posted with users' names and whether or not you will accept items with the user's name not published (but known to you).

- If your use of interactive material is extensive, your home page and all pages on which it may appear should indicate that they contain information that you have not posted. If you review material, that should be noted as well.

Data Entry Page	You may have one or more data entry pages on which people can enter data to be posted to your site. You may have gatekeepers in front of these pages—either passwords or restrictions to specific in-house IP addresses. If you make a distinction between internal and external postings, here is where you may do it. (You may allow internal postings to be sent immediately to the site; external postings may require review.)
User Confirmation Page	You should confirm data entry immediately. Ideally, the confirmation should include the information that the user has submitted. Whether it does or not, make it very clear what the user should do to correct the information—or even withdraw it. If this page does not have that information on it, you will have lots of duplicate postings (as people think of one more thing to add); you will also have frustrated people using all sorts of e-mail addresses to take back what they have said.
Review Page (Optional)	If you review postings—either all of them or those from external users—this page allows the reviewer to retrieve all postings with a display status of Pending (or whatever code you provide). Each posting can then be screened and edited; it is restored with a display status of Public or OK. A common set of display statuses is: • OK or Public—for approved postings • Pending—the status for postings not yet reviewed • Hold—a status for postings reviewed and not accepted

- Private—for postings that should be seen only by privileged users.

Review Confirmation Page (Optional)	If you use a review page to screen postings, a review confirmation page should be presented to the reviewer indicating what action has been performed.

Making It Work: Generating Two Types of Traffic

To make your site interactive, you need to generate traffic both from people who are looking at the information and from people who are posting information. Again, depending on your site's goals, this traffic can be generated in a variety of ways.

For an internal site—such as a corporate event calendar—you can cause its use to increase by using traditional techniques. (If the company president refuses to go to meetings not posted on the Web calendar, the first meeting held without the president will probably cause all future meetings to be properly posted.)

For external sites, the usual array of incentives apply. If you want to get a discussion going on your site, offer a random drawing for something your users want; make it based on their postings. If you have the right incentive, the postings will proliferate (perhaps wildly).

Evaluating Your Site

An interactive site can be evaluated on both quality and quantity. If you are providing a community forum or a corporate calendar, it should be easy to determine how relevant your site is. If you are sponsoring a help discussion group; you will quickly be able to tell if people are relying on your site—and recommending it.

You can also evaluate your site solely on quantity—both of visitors and of posters. Be careful, though, since these statistics can be subject to manipulation.

The most important aspect of evaluating your interactive site is doing it: you do not need massive statistics and time-consuming analyses. Pick the metrics that matter to you and follow them assiduously. If traffic and/or messages drop off or increase precipitously, know why that happens.

Summary

Interactive sites are continually updated by users; as a result, your control over the site needs to be exercised at a distance. The choices you make as to who's in charge, the organization and protection of the information, the design of your site, and the site's general maintenance and evaluation are key to controlling and managing the site successfully.

Even more complex than an interactive site, however, is a transactional site. That is the subject of the next chapter.

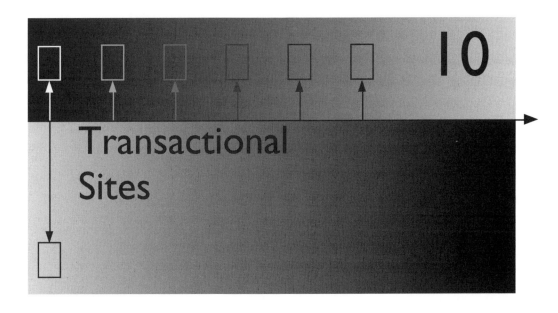

10

Transactional Sites

The success of sites such as amazon.com and the Apple Store has inspired people all over the world to sell goods and services over the Internet. The heart of such sites is their management of transactions—the exchange of items of value.

However, transactions go beyond exchanges of value. The issues raised in the sale of goods and services also need to be dealt with in multipage data entry sites; such sites are used to enter the complex data needed for corporate human resources applications, school course registrations, and a variety of other services.

This chapter provides an overview of transaction processing. The topic is dealt with extensively in Application Servers: Powering

207

the Web-Based Enterprise; *issues of security are addressed in that book as well as in* Database-Driven Web Sites.

Organizing the Information

If someone browses your Web site and gets a mistaken idea of the information there, that normally is not catastrophic. However, if someone agrees to purchase something from you and the wrong item is delivered—or, worse yet, nothing is delivered—that is a more serious issue.

The first step in creating a successful transactional site is identifying and organizing the data.

Identifying the Transaction

Transactions usually involve an exchange of value and frequently entail a sequence of multiple dynamically built Web pages. You can finesse this in some cases by presenting users with a simple HTML form to fill in. They can enter the item they want to purchase, their billing and shipping information, and any special instructions. This form can be sent to a database or via e-mail to a clerk who will fulfill the order.

However, in most cases the user selects one or more items from your site, and they are stored in a shopping cart. When the user is ready to check out, the cart's contents are totaled, shipping is added, and the billing and shipping information is collected.

In complex data entry transactions, a similar process occurs. The user enters data on one page, and as a result of that data, a new page is generated. This is similar to the process in which a shopping cart's contents are totaled—in both cases the data on the first page dynamically controls the data on the next. (Public opinion surveys are frequently structured in this way: if you have a dog, one set of questions is presented; if you have both a dog and a cat, another set of questions is presented.)

Although shopping carts are familiar to users of e-commerce sites, you should consider a shopping cart to be the container of intermediate results. In the case of complex data entry, the shopping cart is the container for the answers to all of a survey's questions; on "checkout" the data is processed. Complex data entry can encompass everything from a detailed consumer survey with hundreds of questions to an online test for students or a help desk inquiry that requires a great deal of structured data to be entered before the inquiry can be accepted for processing.

Storing Intermediate Results

In all cases, there is the need to store intermediate results. This can be done with a cookie on the user's computer; it can also be done with a database on the host. The cookie is simpler, but when a large amount of data needs to be stored, cookies can be problematic.

Furthermore, if a transaction needs to be able to be processed on a variety of computers, cookies will not work. This situation occurs when you allow people to leave a transaction in the middle—some e-commerce sites allow shopping carts to remain filled but not checked out for 90 days.

Committing the Transaction

Transactions are all characterized by a single moment of commitment: the moment at which all of the transaction's processing occurs. This is when value changes hands, when inventory is updated, and when packing slips are generated. Not only does the moment of commitment eliminate the need for storing intermediate results, it also normally entails permanent storage of data (invoices and so forth).

When Does a Transaction Start?

Once a transaction has been started—a complex form starting to be filled in or a shopping cart created—you need to be able to track the transaction all the way to completion. There are two basic approaches to starting a transaction:

1. You can prepare a transaction when someone enters your site for the first time. Particularly if you use a gatekeeper for login purposes, this can be an efficient way to handle transactions. You will screen out people who do not have IDs or who are reluctant to enter the information needed to access your site. However, you will be able to allow them to purchase items with a single click: you have their billing information.

2. The other alternative is to keep the site wide open and collect billing and shipping information at the end. This encourages the type of browsing people are accustomed to in stores.

Be aware that as soon as you start a transaction, you will normally be storing information. Make certain that your privacy policy and your transaction processing are in synch.

Who Are Your Users?

Your choice of when to start your transactions will have a lot to do with who your users are. A mass market store (like the renowned Internet dot-com sites) generally lets people browse and prepare to purchase items with no up-front registration or login. Business-to-business sites, however, frequently are not open to the public and support a login process.

Your users' expectations will help to determine how you structure transactions. For example, on a private network, your users may be logged in at the beginning of their work day, and they may be identified at that time. Complex transactions can be entered at any time during the day without further authentication.

Delivery

The processing of transactions on the Internet is fast. When the transaction can be concluded over the Internet, it, too, is fast. However, when goods need to be shipped or services provided in the real world, the transition from electronic media to trucks or railroad freight cars is the single point at which many problems arise.

One of the most important features your site can provide is comforting guarantees that this chasm has been bridged. All of the major package shipping services have electronic gateways; you can often provide a customer with a package tracking number as soon as the transaction is completed in the electronic world. You can confirm shipping—and intermediate stages of processing—via e-mail. In each case, you are letting the user know that the transition is under control.

When no goods are shipped—in a college course registration process, for example—there may be a delay before the user can get confirmation. Consider adding an in-process file where users can check the status of their requests; this can allay fears. One of the problems with online data entry (particularly by end users who are not chained to their terminals all day) is that you get duplicate data from people who are afraid their first entry has not registered.

Design for a Transactional Database

Designing databases for transaction support is not a new idea: it has been done for decades. There are many books and articles about transactions and database designs to support them.

Two of the most critical considerations are the need for security and reliability as well as the need for speed. Whether on the Web or in a crowded department store, the shopper who spends an hour examining every pair of shoes in the store demands immediate service when he decides to purchase a hat.

Table 10-1 shows a database structure that can be used to support e-commerce transactions. (Note that the symbols next to the table names are explained on page 215.)

Table	Description
Customers†	Each record contains name and address details, account information, credit limits, and other such information; a CustomerID uniquely identifies each one.
Products*	Each record contains information about a product; a ProductID uniquely identifies each one; this is information that generally does not change. (Note: On-hand information is usually not stored here; prices may or may not be.)
Product Status*	Each record has a ProductID that matches a record in the Products table. This is the table with current price, on-hand and on-order quantities, and any other information that changes frequently. (Sometimes this information is stored directly in the Products table.)
Shopping Carts	Each record contains a CartID, a CustomerID, a ProductID, a quantity, and other information needed to support the shopping cart pages. A single shopping cart is retrieved by selecting all records with a given CartID that you generate internally and uniquely. (You cannot use CustomerID, because two people from the same company may be shopping at the same time.)

TABLE 10-1. Tables for a Transactional Database Supporting E-Commerce Transactions

Table	Description
Order Details†	Each record here is similar to (or identical to) a shopping cart record, except that CartIDs are transformed to OrderIDs to identify the contents of each order uniquely. Typically, these records are created by copying all of the shopping cart records with a given CartID and placing duplicates into the Order details table. This is done at checkout time.
Orders†	For each order, a single record in the Order details table with the OrderID uniquely identifying it is generated. This contains information about the order that does not need to be repeated for each item—shipping details, purchase order, etc. This table is sometimes omitted.

TABLE 10-1. Tables for a Transactional Database Supporting E-Commerce Transactions (Continued)

Table 10-2 shows how exactly the same structure can be used to support informational transactions. These can be questionnaires, surveys, or interviews. (Interviews can be used to prepare for help desk actions, meetings, and so forth.)

Table	Description
Users†	Each record contains name and address details; account information, and other such information; a UserID uniquely identifies each one.
Questions*	Each record contains a question or description of data to be entered. Note that each question or data description is in a separate record (and is processed on a separate Web page). This facilitates the construction of a process in which the questions change as the user moves through the site—a useful feature for help desks and complex surveys. Each question or data description contains an ID—QuestionID, for example.

TABLE 10-2. Tables for a Transactional Database Supporting Informational Transactions

Table	Description
Detailed Question Information*	Comparable to the Product status table, this table contains supporting information that may be displayed automatically or on demand with the Questions table information. (Just as the Product status table may be combined with the Products table, so this table may be combined with the Questions table.)
Interviews	Each record contains an InterviewID, a UserID, and a QuestionID. This table is similar to the Shopping carts table. However, instead of a quantity of items, each of these records contains the answer to a question or the data for a data description. Generally, that is textual data. Like shopping carts, a single questionnaire or interview is retrieved by selecting all records with a given InterviewID that you generate internally and uniquely. (You cannot use UserID, because two people from the same company may be entering data at the same time.)
Completed Interviews†	Each record here is similar to (or identical to) an Interviews record, except that InterviewIDs are transformed to CompletedInterviewIDs to identify the contents of each interview uniquely. Typically, these records are created by copying all of the Interviews records with a given InterviewID and placing duplicates into the Completed interviews table.
Interview Details†	For each interview, a single record in the Interview details table with the InterviewID uniquely identifying it is generated. This contains information about the order that does not need to be repeated for each item. This table is sometimes omitted.

TABLE 10-2. Tables for a Transactional Database Supporting Informational Transactions (Continued)

Both of these require an efficient relational database management system—but fortunately these are readily available. From Oracle and DB2 at the high end to FileMaker and Microsoft Access at the lower end, almost any database product on the market today can manage this type of design.

It is important to note that these database tables fall into three categories.

1. Some tables are updated periodically—possibly during the time that transactions are being processed. However, they provide supporting information about products (descriptions and prices) and so can be updated in off-hours. Their information is needed during transaction processing, but it is not updated. These tables have an * next to their names in Table 10-1.

2. Some tables need to be updated quickly as part of the transaction. They are the tables that are updated when people click Buy. In Table 10-1, only the Shopping carts table falls into this category.

3. Finally, some tables (marked with † in Table 10-1) are updated as part of transactions; however, they are updated only once during a transaction—not for each item. Furthermore, their updates are done during parts of the transaction that the user may expect to take a while.

A database design of this sort splits the data into tables so that the data that needs different types of access is together. Tuning the database's performance is made much easier when this is done. Furthermore, keeping the different types of access in separate tables means that you can control parts of the performance yourself: you can do updates in off-hours, for instance. In a database design in which the data is not separated in this way, it is hard to influence performance.

Note in these database designs that intermediate results—the Shopping carts and Interviews tables—are copied to other tables when the transaction is committed. You can also implement a status flag in a single database to accomplish this goal; however, many database designers would prefer this structure since the nature of the committed data is so fundamentally different from that of the in-process data.

Informational transactions collect data for future use. In the case of a help desk, the data may be passed on in the form of an e-mail, or the person solving the problem may retrieve all data from the Completed interviews table and remove it—or change its status—as it is dealt with. It is not uncommon for the information—together with notes, comments, or solutions to problems—to be posted back on a Web site so that people can browse previously answered questions and answer their own. If so, you create a database table with the fields for informational sites described in the two previous chapters.

Designing the Site

Many of the design considerations in the previous two chapters also apply to transactional sites. Here are some concerns for pages specifically found on transactional sites.

Transaction Start Information

This is one of the most important pieces of information you need to provide: you must let the user know when the transaction starts. In other words, the user must know when browsing becomes shopping. Typically, that transition occurs when the user first provides input. That input may be the click on a Buy button, or it may be the click of a button to enter a help desk query. In cases in which customer or user information is entered (as when a gatekeeper guards a site), the user may think that the transaction starts when a password or name is entered—and it may. However, passing the gatekeeper on a transactional site may mean no more than on an information site. In such cases, the transaction starts later on.

In either case, the user must know when mouse clicks "count." You can provide visual cues, such as making the background of all transactional pages similar; you should also provide direct information—such as transaction IDs or shopping cart icons.

Remember that if the user gets lost in the middle of a transaction, the entire transaction is null and void. That may mean that a moment's confusion over the purchase of a minor item can leave the rest of a shopping cart—with hundreds of dollars of merchandise—unattended. It may mean that uncertainty over how to answer a trivial question in an interview may cause a disgruntled user to throw in the towel and stop trying to resolve a technical problem with an online help desk.

Basic Information Page

This is the page displaying the Products table in e-commerce and the Questions table in informational transactions. It presents information for the user to act on—to purchase, or to provide details about.

These pages may be linked to a home page; such is the case in which a handful of products are listed on a home page. They may be indirectly linked to a home page: intermediate category pages (ranges and refrigerators, for example) may stand between the home page and the product pages (in this case, each product page may be an individual range or refrigerator).

Sometimes these pages are presented in a dynamic sequence based on responses to previous pages. For example, someone purchasing a computer at the Apple Store is given the opportunity to look at monitors and printers.

Detailed Information Page

This page lets users specify options such as style, color, size, or flavor for e-commerce; similar degrees of detail can be provided for informational transactions.

This page reflects the data in the Product Status and Detailed question information tables.

Intermediate Results

This page—drawn from the Shopping carts or Interviews table—displays intermediate results. Users should always be able to view intermediate results—and change the data—before committing the transaction.

Sometimes, particularly in consumer surveys, it is desirable not to allow users to go back and change answers.

In cases where the volume of data is low, sometimes the in-process information is stored in a cookie on the user's computer rather than in a database table.

Final Processing Page (Commitment)

This page reflects the Order details and Orders or Completed interviews and Interview details tables. It usually contains a prominent notice to the user to print it. You should always be able to duplicate this page; you may automatically send its contents to the user—and perhaps to yourself or someone within your organization.

Alternatives to Your Own Site

Transactional sites have performance requirements in terms of security, speed, and reliability that may require special support. There are Internet service providers who specialize in this type of support. You need not place your entire site on their hosts; you can place the transactional pages there, leaving the other pages on your own or another server.

Before deciding to support your own transactional site, consider the alternatives—both in terms of price and in terms of the support required. It is very easy to manage a site that works properly; however, you may want to farm out the entire process to get rid of the occasional 2 AM crises.

Performance Issues

Because a single transaction can involve many back-and-forth requests for Web pages and submissions of data, performance is a critical consideration. The nature of shared resources and networks is to have occasional slowdowns: in fact, if you never have to wait to use a shared resource, there is probably too much of it. When you walk into a discount store, you expect to wait in a checkout line with a few people ahead of you. When you walk into Tiffany or Cartier, you expect to see sales clerks waiting around with nothing to do so that you do not have to wait at all.

Your site's performance hinges on many shared resources ranging from the telecommunications network to the Internet itself and the computers serving the site. You can control many of these, but others you need to manipulate indirectly.

For the critical parts of your site, make everything as fast as possible. If you control the computers on which your site runs, consider moving the transactional pages to their own server.

For the parts of the site that you do not control, use every tool and trick that you can think of to make performance acceptable even in times of bottlenecks. "This may take a minute or two" will help users to understand steps in the processing that may be lengthy. Less obvious steps can also improve performance.

If one page will take a particularly long time to load (perhaps because some processing on the host needs to be done before it loads), consider adding additional information to the previous page. If the information is not critical, the user can click a button and wait for the new page to load—while reading information on the previous page. (If the new page loads too quickly, users can use the browser's Back button to go back.)

Performance affects other things, too. To improve performance, many users turn off frames and graphics even though today this may not be needed.

Evaluating Your Site

Transactional sites need to be evaluated on their own criteria in addition to those you use for informational sites. The two most important are performance and reliability.

Performance

Measure performance, but make certain that you have meaningful standards for your site's performance. Because so many diagnostic tools are available on the Web, and since quantitative measurements of so many aspects of sites are available, many people get sidetracked measuring what they can measure rather than what they should measure.

Do you know how quickly a page should load on your site? (This is usually different for each page; you should have standards for each type of page—particularly those that require preprocessing on the remote host.) Do not get involved in measuring pings or other such network performance. That is all very interesting, but to the user sitting at a computer, it is how fast the page loads that matters.

Results

Transactional sites have a built-in evaluation of their results: completed transactions. Track completed and incomplete transactions. The latter can sometimes be more important than the former. If possible, determine why people abandon their shopping carts or their questionnaires. Sometimes the problem is yours; other times it is theirs. You may have to look manually for patterns here.

Summary

The most complex sites are transactional: not only do they usually involve the exchange of value, but they also require a number of interactions between the user and the site for completion. This chapter has outlined the issues involved as well as the database structures that can support such sites.

Now it is time to move on to the high-level site design that incorporates all of the issues involving pages, sites, and types of sites that have been presented in this chapter.

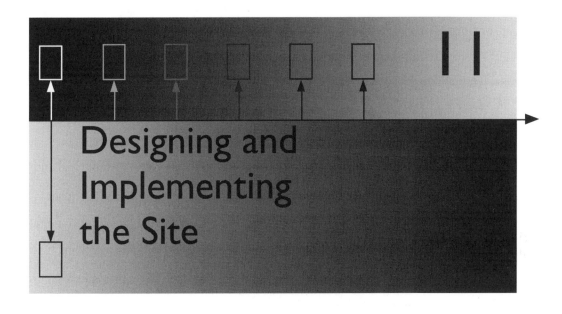

Designing and Implementing the Site

This chapter covers the mechanics of actually designing and implementing the site—putting into practice all of the issues and technologies described previously in the book. For people on the Web, your site is your Web-based enterprise. For people who deal both with your bricks-and-mortar presence and with your Web presence, the site is a part of your organization—frequently the most important part since it is what they deal with in their own home or office.

Designing sites is not about drawing pretty pictures and having clever graphics. It is above all about usability; it is also about content. Whether your site is a reference library devoted to the work of a minor poet or the hub of a set of chat rooms or an e-commerce super-store, if people cannot use it—and do not understand why and how they might use it—all of your work goes for naught. Thus, the chapter starts with a structured method for setting your site's objectives.

Setting the Objectives for the Site

As noted previously, there are two themes that run through this book: the need to integrate your Web operations with the rest of your activities and the need to focus on your users and what they want. In both cases, clarifying the goals and objectives of your site is essential.

Note that these goals may be set for the entire site or for sections of it. If you set them for a section of the site, that section should be clearly identified; if it is not, users—and your support staff—will be confused.

There are three definitions you need to create in order to set your site's objectives. Each has parallels in the world of bricks and mortar; however, you normally implement two of them in very different ways on the Web than you do in the real world.

The three definitions are quite simple concepts:

1. **Mission**. What is it that you do?

2. **Scope**. How much of it do you do or who do you do it for?

3. **Place**. How do you do it?

Mission

Setting your mission or overall objective is something that most people and organizations are used to doing. Setting a mission for a Web site is no different.

Scope

Scope defines how much of your mission you do or who you do it to (or for). Scope is something that you consider in the bricks-and-mortar world, but you address it quite differently there. If you run a library, do you cater to the public or to scholars? If you sell clothes, is it the retail or the wholesale market that you serve?

These questions are part of an organization's mission in many cases; however, on the Web, it is important to handle them separately. The reason is that changing the scope of a bricks-and-mortar enterprise is a fairly significant alteration in its activities.

For instance, opening a warehouse to the public (even if only one day a week) requires installing cash registers, providing the means of handling smaller purchases than the usual wholesale lots, and answering questions and providing after-sale support that are normally done by retailers, not wholesalers.

Similarly, changing your marketing area from your town to your entire country normally involves changes in how you market and advertise your goods. Expanding a theatre's audience from a city to a region requires new ways of advertising as well as plans for transportation—either of audience or of actors. Converting a clinic from a general-purpose facility to one focusing on heart disease or allergies requires modifications to staff and facilities.

On the other hand, changing the scope of a Web-based enterprise is often accomplished with little more than a modification to a Web page. In fact, many a Web-based enterprise has arisen from a bricks-and-mortar organization's desire to change its scope.

Without definition, your site's scope is global. You may be an accountant in a one-person office overlooking a valley in Japan; an attorney in Egypt can click the More Info button on your site. Do you want to enter into an e-mail exchange as to the services that you provide? (You might; the point is that you should know whether you do or not.)

The ease of changing your site's scope makes it critical to define it at any given moment. There are issues that make changes to scope complex: national boundaries, for example, can come into play with the transfer of goods and services.

Whether you consider the matter of scope a question of knowing your users and customers, of geographic areas that you serve, or any other criteria, you should narrow the default scope—all Internet users in the world—to your own objectives.

Place

Finally, place refers to how you do what you do. In the bricks-and-mortar world, place is obvious. A shoe store on Fifth Avenue in New York is a very different place from a shoe store on a street in a small village; likewise, a shoe store located in a shopping mall is different from one located in an industrial park or high up in a skyscraper. In each case, people entering the door immediately have an expectation of how they will be treated.

In the real world, place is more or less immutable. Once you have opened your office, shop, or factory, it is there and its physical characteristics are more or less defined for a long period of time.

Like scope, place is easy to change on the Internet. You can redo your Web site without much trouble. It can go from stodgy to trendy and back again with a few changes of graphics. Each change presents a new impression of how you go about what you do.

Little things can contribute to this sense of place. You must watch for them and use them to your advantage. Place in the real world is defined by bricks and mortar; on the Web, it is defined by minutiae.

Putting It Together

Clarifying mission, scope, and place is essential. If even one of these definitions is missing or incomplete, you and your users will be confused. Usually a lack of clarity results in your spending a lot of resources developing pages that are not needed; on the users' side, a lack of clarity results in frustration.

For example, do users send you e-mail messages saying that they have trouble finding information on your site? Do they question the accuracy of your data? If so, is your response to add instructions to your site and to provide more links to authenticate data? These would seem to be reasonable responses. But if your site is designed to be used by urban planners and these queries come from community groups planning parades, do you care? The correct response is not to add instructions or more information to the site; it is to make clear—politely and/or bluntly—that this site is for professional urban planners. (Again, this seems commonsensical. It bears repeating because it has happened more than once—more than many times, in fact.)

Once you have defined your mission, scope, and place, you are ready to proceed with your site's design and implementation. Clearly assess your situation: your goals, your resources, and everything else affecting your project. You may start by designing your site and then preparing an implementation strategy; that is the sequence in which the rest of this chapter is presented.

But it may be appropriate to start the other way around: start by preparing an implementation strategy and design your site around it. It is very common to have mandates to complete projects by a certain date; it is equally common to have budget and personnel constraints. Preparing a site design that will be late or over budget is just a waste of time, and using your design resources to prove that your budget is unrealistic is frequently just an unprofessional exercise in futility.

In many cases, a third way is possible—or necessary. You must plan your design and implementation together. There is a lot to be said for this approach; neither will get out of synch with the other. If a design feature is going to compromise your implementation schedule, you will know it shortly after the feature is proposed, rather than once the entire design is completed and you start a separate implementation project. The disadvantage of such simultaneous work is that it can be more expensive than doing the two projects sequentially. It may involve more meetings and management attention.

Additionally, there is a very real danger that the simultaneous design (with concomitant testing and experimentation) and implementation planning will in fact turn into doing the project. And that translates into developing your site before you have a plan in place.

Design

As repeatedly stressed in this book, you must design your site for your users. Their convenience—not yours—is paramount.

However, there is one area in which you must put your own needs first. When it comes to site design, your site must be maintainable. A design that does not plan for maintenance is worse than no design at all.

The elements of Web site and page design have been discussed previously in this book. This section focuses on putting them together.

Starting Out

Start your design analysis by knowing clearly where you are beginning. Write your definitions of mission, scope, and place in simple declarative sentences.

Also part of starting out is knowing what you have in place. Is there an existing site? Is your Web presence a page on someone else's site? Is a change in domain name or URL address needed for stationery, business cards, or packaging? The answers to these questions need to be in place at the beginning of your design process; they can be killers and gotchas when addressed at the end. (They tend to require a lot of time to answer and resolve.)

Designing the Site's Structure

Your first concern is the overall design of the site's structure. The site's structure differs from site to site. It may consist of a home page and a variety of subsites, each with its index (home) page. Other sites have a combination of subsites and subsidiary pages from a home page. Still others have no subsites (that is, no internal index pages); all pages are linked directly to the home page. Designing your site entails choosing one of these structures and then identifying the major pages and/or subsites.

Very rarely do you have a clean slate: there is often a structure within which you need to work. If you are dealing with an existing organization, the Web site must reflect that organization's structure. In that way, the pages and subsites can be controlled by the comparable constituents of the organization itself. They may not choose to do so, but they will be able to if they (or their management) choose.

Creating a site structure that does not reflect the organization's underlying structure means that the site's development and maintenance must be done by people other than those who normally perform the tasks.

For example, if an organization has a sales department, a customer support department, and a research department, it makes sense to have a Web site structure with those three departments clearly controlling pages and/or subsites.

Note that the constraints of physical locations within an organization do not apply on the Web. Thus, if you want to structure your site based on types of customers—corporate, government, educational, and so forth—you can do so. Your sales department can clearly be responsible for specific pages within each of the site areas. You do not need a sales subsite. As long as there is some clear way to map the organization's structure to the Web site's structure, you are in good shape.

Testing the Site's Structure

Test your site's draft structure for responsibility in two ways:

1. Can you identify the parts of the subsite that each part of your organization is responsible for?

2. Given a page or subsite of your site, can you identify the part of the organization responsible for it?

Plan Your Site's Servers

Your site's structure is logical, not physical. That means that unrelated pages may be located on one Web server and related pages may be scattered among several servers (and even several hosts).

If you know the environment on which your site will run, lay out its subsites and collections of pages so that you know what servers they will run on. Test this part of the structure by listing the steps to take to replace individual pages, subsites, and the site itself. What is the largest section of the site that you can replace in one step?

Testing Your Server Layout

You may need to start an iterative process here. The servers on which your pages are located may dictate a change to the structure. Secure servers used to support online transactions often get in the way of a logical disposition of pages. You may need to do some rejiggering with regard to what pages are where and who is responsible for them.

If you do not have your hardware environment in place, you may have to come back to this later.

Selecting a Site Design

Having planned your site's structure and server layout, you can select a site design. Whether you choose a unified, distributed, or fragmented design, make it a conscious choice; make certain that you know if that design applies to the site as a whole or only to a subsite. (For more information, refer back to "Types of Site Designs" starting on page 158.)

Testing Your Site Design

Test your site design in the same way that you tested the server layout: check to see which pages need to be changed together. Certain types of changes may require that all pages on the site be updated simultaneously: not an ideal choice. However, you may decide that those changes (such as an overall domain name change) occur so infrequently that you can live with that risk. Look not just at the hypothetical problems but at the real ones. Walk through the types of changes that will occur most frequently, and identify which pages will be affected.

Once again, you may need to loop back to the beginning. The design process is iterative—and endless.

Note that this is the first part of the design process that actually deals with graphic design.

Specifying Standard Pages

Identify standard page types that you will have. You will have at least one home page; you may have informational, interactive, and transactional pages. (See "Defining a Web Page's Function" starting on page 145.) Your site may have further types of pages—standard pages for providing information about goods, services, and corporate information.

For each standard page type, identify its function; then select the parts and characteristics that will apply to that page. (Refer to "Looking at a Web Site" starting on page 153 for definitions of individual parts and characteristics.)

Implementing Standard Pages

Standard pages may be implemented using shared code. If so, the HTML should be prepared and published in whatever format is convenient to your project and organization.

In the case of sites that use dynamic pages and application servers, you may need to prepare additional aspects of standard pages—applets, scripts, and so forth.

Testing Your Standard Pages

Test in the same way: plan out the scenarios for making changes to pages throughout your site. You need to walk through not only the process of changing the pages themselves but also the process of changing the standard pages. Remember to consider the likelihood of each type of change.

You may say that a change to a standard page is unlikely, but you must not ever say that it is impossible. To do so will cause you to create a section of the site that is unmaintainable. This will cause a ripple effect as other parts of the site have to work around the unchangeable sections. Before long, your site will be unmaintainable.

Once again, prepare to go back. Everything is up for grabs. You may not have an ideal solution to any single design problem, but your goal is to achieve the best total combination of choices.

Going back is not a waste of time: far from it. The fact that you can go back and repeat parts of the design process should reassure you that you will be able to maintain the site. If, once made, a design choice cannot be revisited, you are courting failure.

Designing the Pages

Finally, you are down to the identification and design of individual pages. Each page is scarcely blank: you know where on the site it will be, what standard page it will conform to, and you know how to describe its purpose.

At this stage, it is important to identify the pages that will be needed if you have not done so before. For each page, complete the design process with whatever is unique to that page.

Watch for problems in creating pages. Until you are certain that the site design is right, you can accommodate problems by changing the site. Misunderstanding and confusion over the site's standards may be just that—or they may reflect an underlying problem with the site itself.

If pages are to be maintained by other people within the organization, frequently it is a good idea to involve them directly or indirectly with the page design.

These are the final components of your site. Their testing is described in the section that follows.

Implementation

There are two aspects to implementing a site: testing and scheduling. This section addresses those issues.

Developing a
Test Suite

Testing is an overlooked area of site design. You need a detailed set of tests that you can perform to test that the site is working properly. The test suite should be repeatable as needed—you should redo it when you make changes to the site.

The test suite should be as detailed as possible, but it must correspond to reality. A test suite that takes 2 days to execute may be feasible for a large corporation; it is not realistic for a one-person office. Preparing a test suite that is too complex is just a waste of time.

The test suite should be shared with the people responsible for the site as early as possible. Stress to them that these are the tests being performed: you will check to see that they pass. If something matters to them and is not being tested, they should update the test suite.

It is not sufficient to test that things work right—you must test that they fail properly. If a user clicks the wrong button, things should not crash. Warning messages should appear where appropriate. This type of testing is very hard to do—if only because the number of ways in which things can fail is so great. You may have to draw the line here: for example, you may decide not to test what happens to a transaction system in the case of a power failure for both client and server. (In such a case, it may not matter.) Once again, remember to budget as much testing as possible, but work within the bounds of reality and reason in preparing your test suites.

Usability Testing

Usability testing—also known as interface testing—tests to see that people can use your site. In large environments, it involves researchers hidden behind two-way mirrors watching people use the software.

Operational Testing

Operational testing tests to make certain that the site works as it should—are the right database tables updated? What happens to abandoned shopping carts? This is the kind of testing that programmers often think of.

Performance Testing

Performance—or stress—testing tests your environment. Can it handle the volume of data you require? What happens if all employees log on to your human resources Web site at the same time?

Performance testing is difficult to do, but it lends itself to automation and modeling. There are software products available that simulate the effect of hundreds or thousands of users requesting specific pages on your site. There are also products that allow you to measure details of your site's performance and then use mathematical models to simulate various performance loads. Since these tools may need to be installed on your Web server, you should work with your ISP or IT department to identify and use them.

People usually come late to performance testing—the issue often comes up when users complain about poor performance. At that point it is usually too late to do anything about it. Having performance goals set out in advance can help.

Scheduling

The other part of implementation is scheduling and project management. In this regard, setting up a Web site is no different from any other management project.

Where Web site scheduling may differ from other projects that you have worked on is in the fact that it is almost always a round-the-clock operation. Except for an in-house Web site that is running only during business hours, your Web site is expected to be available at all times. That means that you may not have off-hours to perform your work. You may need a sophisticated combination of test and production environments so that you can prepare new pages, test them, and then quickly move them into production.

Deciding What Needs to Be Done

The first step in setting up a project schedule is deciding what needs to be done and defining the tasks. Again, this is like other projects except for the 24/7 aspect of Web work. Many tasks will be scheduled in what are considered off-hours. Furthermore, many tasks will be performed off site; after all, the Web is scarcely confined to a single office cubicle.

In defining tasks, take into account that there will often not be someone to answer a question when it needs to be answered. You will need to make tasks self-contained; you will also need to empower people to make choices and decisions on their own.

Assigning Responsibility

Responsibility needs to be assigned, just as in any project. As noted previously, that responsibility may be broader than in other types of projects. However, the critical point is to make it clear who is responsible. In almost all cases, the people in an organization responsible for the business activity should be responsible for the corresponding Web activity. They know the business, and they know how to handle the problems that come up. Separating responsibility for Web operations from responsibility for bricks-and-mortar operations adversely affects both.

Setting Up a Schedule

With tasks defined and responsibilities assigned, set up a schedule and make certain that it is known. Since you may have people working at all hours and in all sorts of places, allowing the schedule to be updated over the Web can be a useful feature.

Using Web development resources to set up an updatable calendar on the Web can be a valuable learning experience.

Going Live

The steps involved in going live are the same for a new site and for a site to which maintenance changes have been made. The issue is explored in the next chapter.

Summary

You may think that the successful launch of a site is the end, but it is only the beginning. Just as a bricks-and-mortar enterprise continually changes and evolves, so, too, your Web-based enterprise undergoes a constant process of change. Some of those changes reflect correction of bugs; other changes are in response to external forces in the enterprise. Still more changes arise as a result of changes in technology—new operating systems, new telecommunications configurations, and so forth. The final chapter of this part of the book helps you plan for the maintenance that is a constant part of the Web-based enterprise.

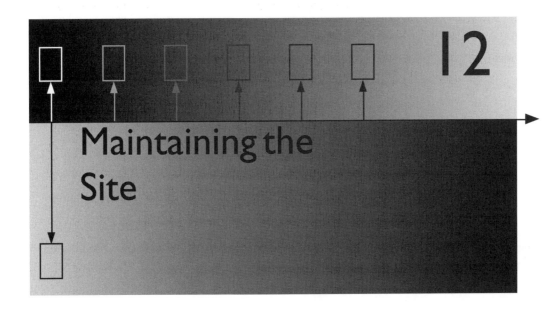

12

Maintaining the Site

Having designed your site and its pages, you can scarcely afford to relax for a moment. Your site is visible 24 hours a day, 7 days a week. Welcome to the world of the Web-based enterprise—a world that never sleeps.

It is also a world that never stops changing. Since everything on the Web can potentially be linked to everything else (and in a sense it is—that is the nature of the Web), there is no static version of the Web at a given moment. Some page or other is always in the process of being updated, and some server or other is in the process of "hiccoughing" or crashing so that its pages are invisible.

Maintenance is an integral part of every Web site. If you are blind-sided by the first problem with the site or the first change that needs to be made, you (and your organization) will probably never recover.

This chapter addresses the major maintenance issues:

- *Managing and changing the site's objectives*

- *Responding to problems*

- *Dealing with problems created by yourself and your organization (such as staffing changes)*

- *Changing the site*

- *Starting over (which you will need to do)*

Maintaining the Objectives

After all the work you have done to define the site's objectives—mission, scope, and place—you need to work hard to keep the site on target. Over time, little accretions of off-target information appear on the site. Just as in an office you may turn the corner of a corridor and encounter an office liaison in flagrante delicto, things happen on Web sites.

One reason for using a Web site register is to keep track of these details for every Web page. As you will see, some changes occur in response to problems: those changes are the ones most likely to cause additional difficulties (this is because of the pressure under which they are made).

However, sometimes the objectives do change. This can come about if your organization changes; it can also come about in response to competitive pressures. Sometimes, the changes arise as the result of discussion or investigation of problems: a redefinition or increased precision in the existing definition may be in order to clear up ambiguity.

Changing the Objectives

If you decide to change the site's objectives, do it systematically. If you have information or a Web page that doesn't fit into your existing site definition, consider the following options:

- Should the information or Web page not be on your site?

- Should you create a subsite for this type of material? (This is the course of action to handle a new product, new branch of the organization, and so forth.)

- Should you redefine part or all of your site's objectives (mission, scope, and place)?

In the last case, you need to make certain that the redefinition applies to existing pages on the site. You may have to delay implementing a change until all pages can be changed; alternatively, you can temporarily create a subsite with slightly different rules.

One way to minimize the need to change the objectives is to make your definitions of mission, scope, and place very simple. The more detailed they are, the more likely they are to change.

Responding to Problems

When problems occur—and they will—you need to be prepared to deal with them. In the world of the Web-based enterprise, that means knowing at every hour of the day and night who is responsible for dealing with a problem.

It also means knowing how you will deal with problems. Most problems need immediate attention. Having as many procedures as possible prepared in advance can save a lot of time in a crisis.

Periodic drills are a good way to maintain readiness. There is never enough time for testing, documentation, and other support activities. However, the more time that you can devote to them, the better your site—and your Web-based enterprise—will be.

Coverage

Coverage becomes a critical issue in these cases. Holidays and weekends are not holidays and weekends on the Web. You can decree that they are, and in some cases that is the end of that.

But you need to watch not just for holidays and weekends but also for staff meetings, conventions, and other occasions on which you and your staff may be incommunicado. Users can (grudgingly) accept that a problem with a site over a weekend is not fixed until the following week, but they are unlikely to understand an outage during the week that is due to a convention about which they know nothing.

Make certain that you keep your coverage schedules up to date as people move around the organization or even leave.

Recognize the Problem

When problems occur, people want action. You may have users (or your boss) yelling at you to do something; you may even be given (often conflicting) requests and demands to "assist" you in solving the problem.

Problems that need immediate attention involve blood or water that is flowing, fire, and the instability that accompanies earthquakes and high winds. Computer problems typically do not fall into these categories.

The first step is to close the door or otherwise stop the interference. You and the others who will deal with the problem need to assess calmly what is going on.

You should have prepared in advance a structure for dealing with problems. Whether it is a paper-based form, a Web page, or a database, it should contain the information shown in Table 12-1.

Field	Description
Problem ID	Generated by the system (or manually).
Problem Name	Your first description of the problem.
Reporting Data	Date, time, and reporter of problem.
Acceptance	Date and time the problem was accepted. Name of person responsible. (These may be the date and time this report is filled out.)
Person Responsible	This may be more than one person in the case of problems involving Web servers and pages.
Priority	All problems are top priority for the people to whom they happen. Try to make your prioritization as automatic as possible based on the description of the problem.
Preliminary Analysis	User and/or troubleshooter's best guess.
Final Analysis	What it turns out to be.
Steps Taken	All steps taken—successful or not. There may be false leads. Track these. All affected pages, sites, and subsites should be listed (include those removed, changed, or added).

TABLE 12-1. Fields for a Problem Report

Field	Description
Resolution	Date and time of resolution; confirmation that the problem was solved.
Final Problem Name	A name briefly describing the problem.

TABLE 12-1. Fields for a Problem Report (Continued)

As you develop experience with your Web site, you will amass many problem reports. If they are stored in a database, you can easily query them to find similar problems. (You can structure the database specifically for your Web site so that problem reports are very easily searched.)

You may open this problem database to users; you can also use it as the basis of a training manual or list of frequently asked questions.

Immediately attempting to solve the problem will often bypass this critical step and leave you—or someone else—to troubleshoot a similar problem from scratch.

Do not omit the information about false leads and dead ends. This, too, is helpful to future problem solvers. Make certain that everyone recognizes that false leads and dead ends are not reflections on them; you need that information.

Refusing to Accept a Problem

Among your procedures, you need one for refusing to accept a problem. This can be one of the most daunting challenges you will face: you cannot make this one up on the spot.

Can you (or the reporting user) not duplicate the problem? Has the problem report become a request that you guarantee that a problem you cannot replicate will not happen again? This is not an easy promise to make.

Perhaps the user has caused the problem. (Your e-commerce site rejects a credit card because the customer has not paid the bill to a bank.) You need to know how to deal with this. In large organizations where this sort of thing can happen, specific wording is often prepared. In the case of declined credit cards, often people are advised to tell customers to contact their bank or credit card company; they are not supposed to speculate on the reason for doing so.

Note that these procedures may well be in place in other parts of your organization; suddenly Web designers may need to know what people in the credit department have known for years. This is yet another reason for integrating the Web site with the normal operations of the organization.

Analyze, Fix, or Work Around?

Once you have accepted a problem, you need to deal with it. Many people think this is a process of finding the cause of the problem and fixing it.

In many cases—particularly on the Web and in database or network environments—finding the cause is impossible or unnecessary. In the case of performance problems—slowdowns or periodic "hiccoughs" in which things just stop—you may never be able to duplicate the situation.

At every step of the way, consider and reconsider the alternatives. If you see a way out of the problem—and if the problem appears not to be one that will repeat itself—work around it.

It is a good idea to prepare your management for the notion that you may decline some problems and that you may also not analyze every problem. When this is explained in the context of normal operations, it can be accepted. In the heat of a crisis, it may not be.

Invoking Plans

Make as much as possible of your problem solving automatic. Particularly if you have plans for escalating problems—and you should—make certain that you cannot stall by saying "Just give me five more minutes." It is human nature to see a light around every corner; unfortunately, it is not always there.

Changing the Site

Deliberately changing the site is much like responding to a problem. In both cases you need a detailed plan of action.

Scheduling the Changes

You need to go back to the design documents you created in setting up your site. Who uses your site (or the part of it that is changing); how long do you need to interfere with its normal processing? Often changes to computer systems and Web sites are scheduled for nights, weekends, or holidays.

If changes are going to occur and you know this in advance, you may want to notify users (on the site or via e-mail) of the upcoming changes. Certainly, if the site will be unavailable for an extended period or if something will dramatically change, they need to know. Even more important, if a change to your site is likely to cause user software or procedures to break, they must know as soon as possible.

Do not assume that users enter through your home page and read everything on it every day. Your responsibility is not to post the information about an up-coming change; it is to cause your users to know that this will happen.

Staging the Changes

Changes may have to be implemented in stages. These may occur over a period of days or over minutes. During the changes, parts of the site may be unavailable; also, some links may break during the changeover. Know at each stage of the process what will work and what will not. That is part of planning for the site change.

Do not believe that everything will go like clockwork. Feel free to query people to make certain that they have thought of the contingencies and problems that can occur. One of the biggest omissions from planning is the possibility that a new problem might occur during the changes or that the changes might be implemented incorrectly. Unfortunately, these cases are all too frequent!

Dealing with Transactions

A special case exists when your changes will affect pages involved in transactions or the transactions themselves. In an ideal world, you could stop new transactions from starting and wait for existing ones to finish. But what do you do about the e-commerce shopper who receives a phone call and leaves a partially filled shopping cart unattended for 45 minutes?

If transactions are affected in any way by your changes, you should assume that you will break one or more transactions. You can shut down online processing for an entire day to avoid this, but even at the time that you shut it down, you may be stopping a transaction.

Furthermore, you may not know when a transaction is in progress. Because of the delays inherent in network transmission, a transaction may have started just at the moment that you stop the database or otherwise halt online processing.

Testing

Testing is not just part of the development of your site; it needs to be repeated whenever the site changes. If you can isolate the possible side effects of a change, you may be able to perform only part of your test suite. However, remember that in testing you are looking for bugs: the software that you believe affects only one part of your site's operations may be faulty and it may indeed affect other areas.

One approach to the need to retest is to group changes wherever possible. Constantly changing a Web site is an invitation to disaster.

This is one reason to use database-driven Web pages. The changes to the content are handled by databases and standard HTML. As a result, you do not need to test when you change the data on the pages.

Going Live

When a new version of the Web site (or the first version of it) is let loose on the Internet, it is live. People can use it, and you can watch whatever monitors and diagnostics you may have.

Going live can be coordinated with other events—the opening of a store, perhaps, or the appearance of a television commercial. Be very leery of such coordinated events. By the nature of the Web and the Internet, changes may not occur at the moment you think they do.

If you have a coordinated event, consider actually making your site changes in advance. If it involves the announcement of a new site, no one will know that the site actually exists. If it involves the modification of a heavily used site, seriously consider whether such coordination is worth the risk that it entails.

Documentation

Document everything. Make certain that your problem reports are updated when a problem is resolved. They will become your best training and reference resource.

Also make certain that other documentation is updated periodically. Changes may make your original site design documents out of date.

Decide in advance how to let users know of changes—if you do so. If a user may discover that something works today but didn't work yesterday, do you wait for a query or notify your users that something was fixed? Again, this is not something to do on the fly.

Starting Over

Finally, remember that from time to time you do need to start over. The site may grow and need to be split into two or more subsites; your organization may grow—or shrink. "Once and for all" just does not apply to Web sites. Understand this—

and make certain that your users and management understand it.

If starting over is considered failure, it will be an unpleasant and unproductive experience. From the first day that you start to design your Web site, recognize that it is only a Version 1.

Summary

You now have the tools to analyze and design the functional aspects of your pages and the site for your Web-based enterprise. (It may be surprising to you to note how little of the design is graphical.) You also have seen how to implement and maintain the site and its pages.

The final part of this book addresses who actually does all this work.

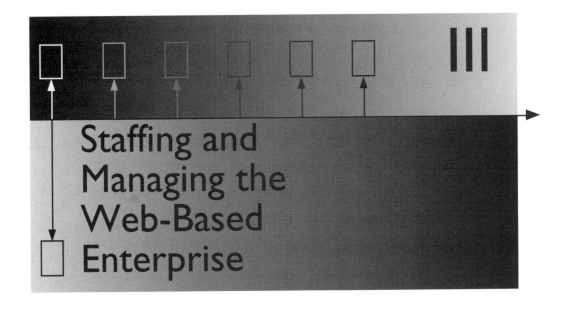

III

Staffing and Managing the Web-Based Enterprise

The first part of this book dealt with definitions and possibilities for the Web-based enterprise; in the second part, you saw how you can set up sites and pages to carry out your objectives. This final part of the book deals with the most important issues of all: staffing and managing the Web-based enterprise.

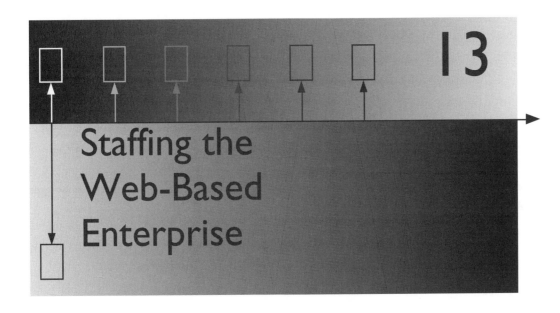

13

Staffing the Web-Based Enterprise

This chapter focuses on the people you need to staff the Web-based enterprise. It is not about hiring programmers or Web-page designers; it is about all of the people in your organization. (Remember that it is the successful integration of a Web initiative with the rest of an organization that makes success possible.)

First, you will find a brief section that addresses a temporary issue: the fact that the widespread use of the Web is barely a decade old and that experience—both at an individual level and in enterprises—is scarce. Next, you will find the staffing options available to you outlined. In the heart of the chapter, you will find sections on resumes, job descriptions, and performance appraisals: this will help you read (and write) the appropriate documents.

The key to building a successful Web-based enterprise is integration of the Web operations with traditional activities. This integration requires a balance between the two types of activities, and that balance is extremely hard to achieve. Err too much on the computer side and you turn into a computer company, forgetting what it is that you were supposed to do for your customers, clients, and the public. Err too much on the other side, and you wind up with a Web operation that limps along held together with electronic versions of tape and baling wire.

Making It Up as It Goes Along

The first draft of the proposal for what became the World Wide Web was written in March of 1989. At that time, commercial use of the Internet was just beginning.

The Internet was originally developed with United States government funding of several networks (including ARPANET) that were available for research, education, and government purposes. The National Science Foundation funded NSFNet from 1986 to 1996 as a 56 kBps backbone for the Internet that ran across the country. Commercial use of that backbone was not allowed. However, during that decade, commercial network providers built a multitude of high-capacity network components and so it was possible to route commercial messages around NSFNet, thus opening the Internet to commercial use.

The pioneers of the commercial use of the Internet and of the World Wide Web are around today. The people with the most Internet and Web experience garnered that experience by trial and error (books such as this one were not available 10 years ago). Furthermore, that experience was gained in a very different environment: everyone was experimenting, and everything was new.

The transformation of the Web from a place of experimentation to an integral part of life has happened remarkably quickly. The skills that were needed 5 or 10 years ago are not necessarily needed today; in fact, some of them are detrimental to building and maintaining Web sites today.

The integration of the Web with other aspects of life is proceeding quickly. During this period of transition, there are divisions between Web users and other people; training—and retraining—is needed that will not be needed in the future. At the individual level, several troubling responses to this transition and transformation of traditional ways of working can be seen. Each response has potential problems—and for each, there are steps that you can take to minimize problems. The key is to recognize these responses for what they are: legitimate concerns that go far beyond your organization. Many organizations come to believe that they have unique problems in implementing Web strategies; few do.

"I Have People Who Do That"

Opting out of the Internet and Web activities in an organization is a choice. Unfortunately, when it happens at a managerial or supervisory level, it sends a message that is hard to overcome. Particularly if you are adhering to the central point of this book—the integration of the Web with other activities in the organization—this statement is dangerous.

Maintaining a hands-off attitude further damages the organization by placing decisions in the hands of technologists who may not have the perspective and experience of the (nonparticipating) managers. People may laugh about making Web sites "management proof" so that "even" a manager can figure them out, but the issue is serious.

On the other hand, the active participation of key managers and supervisors can make a Web endeavor succeed. In fact, the adoption of new technologies frequently proceeds from the top down.

It is not widely remembered that in 1960, executives normally had telephones, but they rarely placed their own calls. (Some executive telephones in fact had no dials.) When President Kennedy had a multiline telephone installed in his office in the White House, executives around the world suddenly started to place their own telephone calls.

"Please Let Me Do It"

The other extreme can also be dangerous. Beware of employees—at any level—who jump at the prospect of designing or maintaining Web sites at the expense of their own jobs. Integration of Web sites with the rest of the organization means using each person's skills and experience appropriately. Over-eagerness can be just as much a danger as rejection of the technology.

Clearly, a balance needs to be struck. It may be best for all concerned for an accountant to have a change of career to become a Web page designer. What matters is that this be recognized. No matter how you look at it, you will probably need to hire either a Web page designer or a new accountant.

"I'm Too Old"

Some people are reluctant to change their ways. This, too, is a temporary situation as it applies to the Web. Young children today do not know a world without the Internet; in most schools, basic computer skills are taught in the earliest grades.

For people in the transitional generation, these can be frightening years. They may fear that unless they jump on the rapidly moving trend, they will be left behind. People who are frightened are not good employees.

Notwithstanding the need to integrate the Web into the organization, remember that not everyone needs to be heavily involved with the technology. You can—and often should—customize job descriptions to accommodate valuable people inside the organization with the experience that outside Web developers will never have.

Retraining the "Experts"

As noted previously, the people with the most experience in the Internet and the Web may not have relevant experience for today's work. It is no longer a time of invention; it is now a time of adherence to standards. Someone who refuses to work within the confines of the maturing Web is no less a problem than someone who refuses to work with the new technology at all.

"I'm Afraid"

There is more than a little fear involved with creating a Web-based enterprise. For a startup company, there is the fear of failure; for existing companies, there are legitimate fears that the new enterprise may not succeed and that it may even bring down the parent company itself.

You cannot overestimate the magnitude of the changes when an organization integrates the Web into its operations. Recognizing the fact that fear can be rampant can help you to deal with it and prevent problems.

Note that all of these responses to the integration of the Web into organizations are a result of the transition to a pervasive Web environment.

Getting the Job Done

It is all well and good to talk about integrating the Web into your operations, but who is going to do the work? There are a number of ways to find people to do the work. These range from outsourcing to using consultants, existing staff, and various combinations.

One consequence of the youth and dynamism of the Web world is the fact that there are no clear-cut lines of demarcation between different types of operations. Terms such as "Web hosting" and "webmaster" have different meanings to different people; as a result, comparing products and services is difficult. Rely on details, not jargon, to evaluate your choices.

Outsourcing

Companies often outsource parts of their operations. Order fulfillment and warehousing are commonly outsourced; similarly, building maintenance, legal affairs, and accounting are outsourced in many cases.

Outsourcing has benefits in that you do not need to maintain staff and support facilities for the operation involved. It has dangers in that a critical part of your organization's operations may not be under your control.

When it comes to Web operations, outsourcing can make sense in some cases. Integrating the Web with an organization's operations must be done at management and operational levels; it does not require that a company run its own Web servers or maintain its own Web pages.

Develop an outsourcing strategy. Know what it is that you are outsourcing. Outsourcing Web site design is very different from outsourcing operations of your Web site.

If you are considering outsourcing, there are three general routes to take:

1. International consultancies

2. Regional Web development companies

3. Other vendors

International Consultancies

Major consultancies have grown out of what were originally accounting companies. These companies provide management and operational services to large organizations. They generally have multinational operations and can provide a wide range of services.

Because these organizations themselves are global in scope, they often have dealt with some of the problems that large-scale enterprises face with the Web and telecommunications. This can be an advantage. Similarly, the resources on which they can draw quickly can be vast.

A disadvantage can be the fact that the cost and overhead of these consultancies can be high. (Some people complain that they never leave an organization once they have arrived.) They also can be somewhat less prone to innovation than smaller companies. Their respect for precedent can be high.

If your organization has an existing relationship with an international consultancy, consider expanding that relationship to the Web. However, be fully aware that this is not just another accounting operation; make certain that they understand your goals for your Web-based enterprise.

Regional Web Development Companies

In every part of world, regional Web development companies provide customized outsourcing for organizations. One important advantage of using one of these companies is that they frequently have a very good understanding of regional telecommunications issues; they also generally know regional organizations (such as banks) that can provide necessary ancillary services.

On the negative side, companies based solely on Web development mutate frequently. The regional company that specializes in your region can pick up and (electronically) leave the area overnight. In addition, they may be more focused on the technology than on your business operations.

Other Vendors

In addition to consultancies and Web development companies, other vendors can provide all or part of your outsourcing needs. Advertising agencies provide Web design as part of their services; telecommunications companies provide remote hosting of network servers.

Using Consultants

Consultants are generally individuals who work directly with your organization. They are not on your payroll, and they (or their organization) pay for their benefits. They may work for a day or two—or they may work for years and appear to be employees.

Consultants are common in the computer world. In hiring one, you need to make certain from the beginning how much autonomy the consultant has. If you are following the principles in this book, you want tight integration of your organization with its Web operations. In such a case, you want a consultant to listen very carefully and work towards your goals. You do not want someone to come in and put up a Web site that looks like the Web site that was put up for another organization last week.

Making this clear at the beginning can save a lot of grief later.

In-House Resources

The easiest way to integrate Web operations with traditional operations is to do it in house. The disadvantage of doing so is that you may reinvent the wheels of the Web as your staff experiments and discovers what outsiders have already learned.

Step back from the glitz and glamour of the Web and evaluate what it is that you want to do and what strengths your organization has—or wants to have. If you run 24/7 computer operations, adding a Web server is not likely to be a significant burden. If your computerization consists of word processing and the occasional simple spreadsheet, adding a Web server may be a disaster.

Plan not only for what you want to do now but for where you want to be when the dust settles. Using consultants to help you develop your Web site can be very useful; but make certain that everyone understands whether that is to be a long-term arrangement or whether in-house staff are to take over.

Telecommuting

No matter where the staff comes from, you will need to address the issue of telecommuting at some point or another. One of the great virtues of the Internet is its ability to reduce the constraints of time and place on the way people live and work. However, there are such things as meetings, and there is something to be said for soaking up atmosphere and actually talking to users over lunch.

To get the most out of telecommuting, make certain that everyone understands what needs to be done and what needs to be done on site. Be creative: one way to solve the meeting problem is simply to reduce the number of meetings.

Resumes for the Web-Based Enterprise

Nowhere is the transitional nature of the Web-based enterprise more evident than in resumes. Job descriptions look to the future, and performance appraisals deal with the immediate past. Resumes, though, deal with all of an applicant's life to date. You will not find someone with 10 years of experience as a Web designer; you need to find relevant prior experiences, skills, and character traits that may provide you with the person you need. (Or, if you are writing your own resume, you can explain how your experience is relevant to a Web-based enterprise.)

The integration of the Web with an organization's bricks-and-mortar functions means that everyone needs to be aware of Web issues. You can read this section as applying to members of a Web team; however, these questions need to be considered for almost every new hire in a Web-based enterprise.

Obviously, you need to consider a wide range of issues in screening resumes. Those in this section are particularly relevant to a Web-based enterprise; furthermore, a different perspective may inform your view when you consider the needs of the Web-based enterprise.

Reviewing resumes not only matters when you are hiring new people; you need to review the resumes and work experiences of existing staff members when planning for their roles in a Web-based enterprise.

Experience

Resumes explicitly list a person's experience—job related as well as educational. In addition, resumes often list community, social, and volunteer activities that help you to understand more about the applicant. These additional activities are particularly important because relevant work experience at Web-based enterprises is likely to be scarce.

The two most basic types of experience are technological and business.

Technology

In looking for technological experience, look for people with experience with the type of technology that you are using. If you have a particular type of computer system or if you use a certain Web server or Web authoring tool, hiring someone who has used those exact products can be a seductive thought. However, remember that computer systems change and product choices evolve over time. You may be locking yourself into an environment that is not optimal.

If you need immediate help with specific technologies, consider consultants and other contract workers.

Business

Someone who understands your operations (or your type of operations) can be much more valuable than an experienced technologist. In general, this type of domain knowledge is harder to acquire than a knowledge of technology.

Ideally, you need people with experience in your business or in the technology you are using and with a strong interest in the other. Here is way those volunteer and community activities come into play.

Skills

In addition to experience, you look for specific skills. In some cases—such as hiring new entrants into the workforce—there is no experience to speak of, and you need to focus entirely on skills.

Communications Skills

The Web is a communications medium. The primary skill you need to look for is the ability to communicate. Unfortunately, you cannot rely on a resume as a sample of an applicant's communication skills—many resumes are worked over by many hands to improve them.

Remember that the communication skills that you need are of two kinds: you need people who can communicate with other members of a team, and you also need people who can design and implement the communications on a site. In the first case, you need people who speak (and listen) well. In the second case, you need people who are adept at using words and graphics to communicate a message. (Spontaneous conversation is almost irrelevant in the second case.)

You cannot get around poor communications skills. Do not start a project which is, after all, about communications with a problem on that score.

Design Skills

You may need to hire people for a Web team with design and graphics skills. If you have not done this before, it can be daunting. You will probably see samples of applicants' work. Look for effective communication—do not look for works of art. "Pretty" is not what you need.

Ask an applicant to describe and critique artwork. You can pick an ad from a magazine (or a Web site's design); you may also be able to select one or more samples of the applicant's work. Listen to the discussion. (This is also a test of communication skills.) Listen for a functional approach to design; listen (negatively) to decorative notions.

For example, in analyzing a home page, a designer might focus on its "look." Another designer might focus on how the layout can accommodate the varying information that will appear on the page over time. Take the second applicant.

Design skills are not restricted to Web page creators. Increasingly, design skills are needed by people preparing presentations, creating spreadsheets, and developing end-user productivity solutions.

Technology Skills

As with design skills, you may be forced to evaluate skills about which you know little. Fortunately, the process is almost exactly the same. If an applicant wallows in technological mumbo jumbo, see if you can find a glimmer of concern for the workings of your operation. Why the technology matters and what it means to you and the user are what should be uppermost in everyone's minds.

Technological skills can be just as distracting as pretty art-work in a designer's portfolio. Look for relevance and concern with the process.

Traits

Finally, you need to look at personality traits that will help the individual work in your organization. Four particular traits are particularly relevant to a Web-based enterprise.

Experimentation

You need someone who is willing to experiment. Few Web pages are right the first time, and few Web-based organizations do not need to redo their Web sites (repeatedly). Someone who needs stability and is reluctant to try new or different approaches may not be the best choice for a Web-based environment—at least during this transitional phase.

Tenacity

You also need tenacity and the ability to know when to stop experimenting. Sometimes, experimentation comes with an inability to finish things up neatly.

Learning

You need people who can learn. Precisely because you will not find people—particularly senior people—with years of relevant experience, you need people who are open to new ideas.

Learning is not just a matter of knowing how the Web works; people need to be able to learn by watching how a Web site is used and what mistakes are made. Saying that the user just does not know where to click to find needed information avoids the possibility that the site is not properly designed and that the information in question is effectively hidden.

Collegiality and Sharing

The Web is a collaborative environment. The essence of the Web—its links—is all about breaking down barriers and moving around. People who like to be in control—whether of a Web site or of other people—can be difficult on a Web team and in a Web-based enterprise.

Telecommuting/ Independent Work

Finally, you should consider whether someone can work alone—possibly by telecommuting. A Web-based enterprise functions on Web time—that is, 24 hours a day, 7 days a week, and quickly at all times. This requires flexibility on everyone's part.

Job Descriptions for the Web-Based Enterprise

While all job descriptions in the Web-based enterprise encompass a degree of computer and Web literacy, some job descriptions are specific to the Web site and its operations.

Job descriptions and titles are changing rapidly in this area. Here are some of the most commonly used and how they may fit into your organization.

Webmaster

A webmaster is often the organizer and manager of a Web site. Originally the single person who put up and maintained a Web site, a webmaster now is frequently more of a coordinator.

Whether as coordinator, manager, or sole practitioner, a webmaster's job description typically includes the following:

- Overall responsibility for the Web site.

- Supervision of Web team—both in house and consultants.

- The webmaster may or may not be responsible for site operations and maintenance of the Web server. The description should make that clear.

- The webmaster may be responsible for coordinating and selecting vendors of Web services.

- Design of the Web site.

- Testing.

- Management of the site—updating, adding, and deleting pages as needed.

- Management and maintenance of the site's hardware and software operations.

- Recommending upgrades to hardware and software (including the Web server).

- Managing security on the Web site.

- Compliance with copyright law and privacy policies.

- Keeping links working (changes on other sites can break your own links).

- Providing performance metrics about the site's availability as well as results (purchases made, for example).

- The webmaster may also be responsible for helping to develop enterprise-wide Web usage policies including privacy, personal Web pages, and links to other sites.

- In some organizations, the webmaster is also responsible for assigning userids and passwords to internal users.

- Keeping up with technology—evaluating new advances and recommending changes in implementation of the Web site.

The webmaster normally reports to a manager who is responsible for the Web site and/or Web operations. This may be a position such as a vice president of Internet operations or it may be a position such as president of the company. (Webmasters also sometimes report to Web producers or to senior webmasters.)

Web Producer

A Web producer is typically responsible for the content of the Web site. A common distinction between webmasters and Web producers is that webmasters are responsible for operations of sites and Web producers focus more on their development. However, as with everything in this field, the distinctions are often arbitrary.

Typical responsibilities include:

- Development of content.

- Editing of content developed by others.

- Managing a Web development team.

- Working with (sometimes supervising) programmers developing scripts and other applications to interact with the Web site.

- Monitoring competitive sites and enterprises.

- Keeping up with technology.

Some or all of the webmaster's responsibilities may also be assigned to the Web producer—particularly during the development phase of a site's existence.

Note: Just about every site has an identifiable webmaster; not all sites have a Web producer.

Web producers report either to webmasters or to the same managers to whom webmasters report.

Web Engineer

Web engineers develop programs and scripts that are used to interact with legacy systems, databases, and forms. They may be programmers assigned to a Web team, or they may be members of a computer department who work on an as-needed basis.

Note that some programmers feel that writing CGI scripts and programs to support the Web is demeaning and trivial. By the same token, some Web page designers feel that they can toss off such scripts and programs without understanding the principles of programming—including error checking, testing, and the like. Fortunately, the simplicity of many of these scripts and programs is a saving grace, but you should be aware that you are entering a potentially dangerous area.

Typical Web engineer responsibilities include:

- Development and maintenance of CGI scripts.
- Development and maintenance of interfaces to legacy systems and databases.
- Serving as an interface between legacy systems and database staffs and the Web team.
- Implementing—or helping to implement—changes to environmental software on the Web server.
- Testing.
- Keeping up with technology.

Web engineers report either to webmasters or Web producers or to a separate corporate information technology department.

Site Manager

A site manager is responsible for the content of the site once it is developed. The site manager fulfills the maintenance duties related to content as described under Web producer.

Site managers (if they exist) report to webmasters in most cases.

Operations Manager	The operations manager manages the hardware operations and the Web server. Typically, an operations manager reports either to the webmaster or to a corporate information technology department head. The operations manager fulfills those tasks related to maintenance that are described for the webmaster.
Graphics Artists and Writers	Working for either webmasters or Web producers, these people actually produce the words and graphics for the site. They are frequently freelancers or consultants. They also often are on loan from other areas of the enterprise. They should have some basic training in specific demands of working on the Web (such as Web-safe palettes).

Performance Appraisals for the Web-Based Enterprise

No matter what the job titles are and what structure there is to a Web site's team, certain elements of the work can be evaluated when it is time to do so. Here are some of the key evaluations that need to be made—for someone or other. (This list can also serve as a reminder of tasks that need attention in running a Web site and a Web-based enterprise.)

Does It Work?	The simplest performance appraisal measurement is whether the site works or not. Are goods and services sold; is information conveyed? The more concrete the performance metrics, the better. (See "Metrics and Performance" starting on page 284.)

Are People Happy?	The feedback from the site—or from an individual's part of a site—provides an indication of whether or not people find it easy to use. E-mail complaints are easy to generate; you often will know how the site is being received.
Knowledge Sharing	Partly because this field is so new, islands of knowledge crop up. It is important to let people know that their performance appraisal includes their sharing of knowledge—that is, they will be downgraded if they create fiefdoms of private information.
Availability	Is the site—and the individual—available when needed? In order to support 24/7 operations, many people telecommute or work nontraditional hours. If they do so, it is partly their responsibility to make themselves available at the times and locations to which they have agreed. Flextime is not vacation time.
Keeping Up with Technology	Every member of a Web team needs to keep up with technology. Keeping up with technology does not mean adopting each new feature and tool; it means knowing about the advances and deciding which ones are relevant. An overeager adoption of each new advance can lead to a destabilized site and disgruntled users. On the other hand, stomping your little feet and shouting that a technology—such as frames—is no good really will not get you very far.
	Beware the temptation to pick a technology and stick with it. People can get very cozy with their favorite tools; everything needs to be questioned on a routine basis.

Keeping Up with the Enterprise	Members of the Web team need to stay abreast of the enterprise's goals and operations. Integration between the Web and the rest of the enterprise requires a lot of effort. Outreach—from both sides—needs to occur on a regular basis. This can be difficult when a Web team consists of people who see themselves more as "Web" than as enterprise. Knowing that they will be evaluated on this can help address this issue.
Keeping Up with the Business	Similarly, members of the team need to keep up with the environment in which the enterprise functions—be it government, manufacturing, service, or operations. For people who consider themselves "techies," this can be a lot of work; however, as with the previous case, it is important to let people know that it matters.
Appraising and Managing Superstars and Millionaires	Because of the nature of the Web business today, some people are reluctant to say or do anything that might cause Web team members to leave or be unhappy. This is an issue that warrants a lot of thought. On balance, treating people fairly and honestly and making clear what their job responsibilities are and how they will be evaluated is often the best—and only—way to address this issue.

Summary

As the Web has evolved, jobs and job descriptions have evolved with it. No longer do Web page designers need to know HTML: in fact, HTML coders may be at a disadvantage when placed against Web designers who use graphically oriented authoring tools such as DreamWeaver.

This chapter has provided an outline of the jobs, job descriptions, and performance metrics that you need to manage a Web-based enterprise. Of course, in such a fast-moving world, no one can stand still. The next chapter addresses training for the Web-based enterprise staff.

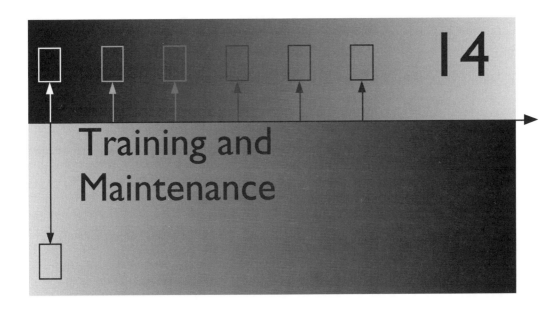

14

Training and Maintenance

If you think that putting up a Web site is the goal you are after, you will either be unsuccessful or be in for a disappointment. The Web-based enterprise requires ongoing training and maintenance of its operations. This chapter focuses on those issues.

Training today means evolving along with the Web itself. Whereas there are standards and "best practices" for many other endeavors, they do not exist fully for Web-based enterprises. In part, this is due to the novelty of the Web; it is also due to the significant changes in the Internet—particularly the growth of broadband communications that make enhanced media such as video possible.

Even once—if—the technologies settle down, there will still be a need for training and reevaluation. First, this chapter addresses the major training issues—the different needs to be addressed and the types of training available. Next, an overview of maintenance operations is provided. Evaluating the performance of a site and of a Web-based enterprise requires knowing what it should be accomplishing and how it should be doing it. That is covered in the section on metrics and performance. Finally, various ongoing issues are explored.

Training Needs

Training for the Web-based enterprise falls into two broad areas: training in technology and training in business operations. Each type of training should recognize the other's needs. Remember, the goal is integration of Web and other activities in the organization.

Note that training and keeping up with advances are important parts of every job description in the Web-based enterprise. Each job description should specify an annual amount of training that a person is expected to receive. You need to make it clear whether the individual is responsible for selecting or suggesting training or whether it is a supervisor's role to do so.

Technological Training

Technological training is of two types:

1. People need to be trained in the technologies they are using. This is initial or setup training.

2. People need to be trained in advanced features and in new advances. This is ongoing training.

Because of the nature of technological changes, you need to recognize that newly trained people will frequently know different material than will those trained in the past. Pioneers' knowledge frequently becomes outdated as the latecomers to technology learn new skills.

Not only does the technology itself change, but the evolution of technology within an organization changes; the training needs for an organization setting up a Web presence are very different from those of an organization that did so several years ago.

Business Training	Most organizations have ongoing training programs for their operations and in issues that affect them. As an organization moves to integrate the Web with its operations, these programs all need to be reevaluated. Policies and procedures change to accommodate technology; furthermore, the technology raises new issues.

The objectives of a Web-based enterprise and its sites—mission, scope, and objective—become part of the business training, along with the new vocabularies of the Web.

Types of Training

Particularly if your organization has a training division in place, you may need to revamp it and to broaden its horizons. There are a number of mechanisms for training staff and management that you can use. Some of them are probably used already; others may be new to you.

Organizations tend to focus on specific types of training—sometimes for personal or historical reasons. Thus, you will find one company that always attends trade shows but never sends people to seminars or conferences; at another company, you may find the reverse. Considering experimenting with different types of training.

Classes

Formal classes both in technological issues and in business issues are available from a broad range of providers. A danger with some classes is that they are developed and then frozen; each iteration is basically the same as the past. You need to make certain that the material being taught is still relevant and that the latest information that you need is included.

Seminars and Conferences

Seminars and conferences provide opportunities to learn material that is usually updated fairly frequently. (Often these presentations are revised each year; some are given one or more times over the course of a year and then replaced with other material the following year.)

These events provide not only an opportunity to get the latest information but also a chance to meet with other people in the field. They typically range from 1 to 5 days in length and are often held in hotels and other meeting centers.

Trade Shows

Trade shows provide training opportunities in their exhibits as well as in seminars and conferences that may accompany them. Trade shows provide the absolute latest information—often including just-announced and preannounced products. They also frequently provide special offers.

Trade shows provide a particularly good source of training if you attend as an exhibitor. Customers and potential customers will be glad to let you know what they like or do not like about your organization. Go prepared to collect this information. It may be anecdotal, but it is valuable.

Using the Web

A variety of training opportunities are available on the Web. They range from materials that can be downloaded to online training programs complete with evaluations and tests. In addition, the Web itself is a training opportunity. Learn from other Web-based enterprises and their sites. Set aside time for people to surf the Web, to identify issues that are raised on other Web sites, and to talk about what they see. Do not reinvent the wheel.

One of the hardest points to make to management is that disciplined Web surfing is essential to Web developers. It certainly looks like a waste of time, but it should not be.

Mass/Popular Media

Do not ignore the traditional media as a training resource. You will find articles about constructing Web sites in daily newspapers. Sometimes the tips are just as valuable as those in a $1000-a-day seminar.

Watch also for evaluations of Web sites (including your own) in the media. Look for what is appreciated and for what is not. Look, too, for what is misunderstood. Avoid the mistakes of others.

Consultants and Trainers

Consultants and trainers are available to customize training for your staff. In setting up training, work with the consultant and trainer to make it clear what your needs are. A trainer or teacher should not stand up in front of your employees and say, "If your site uses frames…." That information should be available to the trainer beforehand.

Make it clear to the trainer (and to yourself) if you intend to reuse the training materials.

In-House Trainers

You may develop in-house training resources. This can be done by hiring a consultant or train-the-trainer, by hiring someone with the necessary skills, or by sending someone to the appropriate classes.

Using in-house trainers may require that your staff wear two hats. You may wind up with junior staff teaching senior management—and not everyone is comfortable with that. Also, trainers need skills at communicating as well as knowledge of their material. Those two skills along with other job-related skills may not be present.

Nevertheless, in-house trainers frequently provide the best and most customized training.

Credentialed Training and Certification

There are certification programs that lead to credentials for people skilled in certain areas and in products. Sometimes this is just an opportunity for a vendor to get a mailing list of sales contacts; in other cases, it is a very valuable program that can also provide opportunities for direct access to a company's resources.

Consider whether certification or credentialed training is appropriate for your operations. You can offer this as a service to your customers and users in some cases.

Books

Last but not least, books and other reference materials on technology and the Web-based enterprise allow individuals to pursue the information that they need when and how they need it.

Where to Train

Training needs to be done away from the distractions of routine work. This may mean reading a book in a library; it also may mean doing off-site training. The cost of sending someone to a conference or seminar may be daunting, but you simply do not learn well when the phone is constantly ringing.

Include travel expenses in your training budget.

The Training Problem

Some people fear that training their staff is a bad investment since they may then take the training and leave. There are even proposals that people reimburse their employers if they leave within a certain period of time after a training program.

If you are concerned about these issues, you have bigger problems. If you do not trust your staff (or they do not trust you), training is unlikely to help.

Maintenance

Web sites need to be maintained. Just as you arrange to have the floors swept and the furniture dusted, you need to arrange for the routine maintenance of a site. To pursue the metaphor, there are other routine—but less frequent—maintenance tasks such as redecorating and repainting; you need to include those in your project plans and budgets.

There is no point in putting up a Web site if it is not going to be maintained. Unfortunately, the computer industry has a very long history of concentrating on the initial sales and implementations of systems and ignoring their maintenance.

Versions and Cycles

Assume that every page needs to be identified not only by its creation and modification dates but also by versions and cycles or some similar notation. This notation consists of at least two numbers, such as 2.03. A major change to the page (often a change to the entire site) is reflected in the first number—2. The second reflects minor modifications such as corrections of misspellings that may be generated.

By using two-part notations such as this, you can describe a site's version—2—without worrying about specific modifications. Thus, pages with version/cycle values of 2.03, 2.21, and 2.00 would all represent a particular version of a Web site.

Implement this at the beginning. All too often it is done for the first revision, and you find yourself in the awkward case of assuming that pages without version/cycle information are from version 1 when they may actually simply have missing information on them.

Responding to Problems

Maintenance and managing problems are covered in both *Database-Driven Web Sites* and *Application Servers: Powering the Web-Based Enterprise*. In addition to the points made in those books, consider the additional points in this section.

Automate Responses

Make as much as possible of your problem solving automatic. One a problem is reported, the steps involved in assigning it to someone to be solved and in coping with it should require as little judgment as possible. This is because it is human nature to think that just one more effort will solve the problem— and before you know it half a day has gone by.

Coverage

This may be your organization's first excursion into Web time—the 24/7 world in which there are no off-hours. This means that there must always be coverage of your systems: you need to start to keep track of the people who are responsible at all times. This does not mean that every member of your Web team or the business support team needs to be available at all times; it does mean, though, that you need to identify who must be available (by job title or description) and which person will be available at any given moment.

You may encounter problems over holidays; there may also be problems during periods of trade shows and conventions when almost all of your staff is away. For these times, you need to consider alternative forms of coverage ranging from telecommuting to temporary employees.

Integrate Problem Solving with Development and Maintenance

The information derived from solving problems is grist for the mill of development and maintenance. Make certain that your feedback loop is closed so that problems not only are solved but also are prevented in the future.

Dealing with Changes

Part of maintenance consists of dealing with planned changes to your Web site and your operations. Some of these changes are highly predictable—for example, you may have seasonal variations in your product line. Others are less predictable but quite sweeping (such as a merger or acquisition that changes your company's name).

The point to remember is that these are to be expected, even if you cannot predict the time or scope of the specific changes. Everything about your operation and your Web-based enterprise needs to be changeable.

Staging and Scheduling Maintenance

When you can predict changes, prepare their implementation carefully and examine all of the ramifications. Pay particular attention to cookies and cached copies of Web pages that may exist. (You may start to prepare for a planned change by clearing caches days or weeks ahead of time so that your changes will appear to occur more or less at once.)

What may seem like a cutover at a single moment to you in fact is a rolling transition on Web servers around the world.

Metrics and Performance

One set of complaints that you will hear is that your Web site is sluggish and experiences slowdowns. No matter how sophisticated it is and no matter how much computer power you have at your disposal, these complaints will occur.

The only way to handle such issues—and they must be handled—is to prepare performance metrics for your operations. This includes not only the Web site, its databases, and its applications but also every aspect of your operation. You are dealing increasingly with people who are distant; a moment on hold on the telephone can seem like an eternity. People are understanding of almost any delay if they are prepared for it. If you tell someone that you will respond to a customer complaint within 24 hours, do so.

Avoid the temptation to measure aspects of performance that do not matter. The best performance measures are the most general: number of items sold, for example. When you start to measure individual mouse clicks, you need to make assumptions about what those clicks mean. When you measure sales, you know what they mean: cash in the bank.

The micromeasurement of performance on Web sites is made possible by all sorts of monitoring and statistical software. An enormous amount of effort can be spent in collecting and analyzing these often irrelevant numbers.

Ongoing Issues

Finally, there is a collection of ongoing issues to which you need to pay attention. They can get lost in the day-to-day work of maintaining your site and running the Web-based enterprise; however, they do need periodic attention.

Experience versus Ruts

As with any job, people need to strike a balance between positive experience and negative ruts. This is particularly true with regard to a Web-based enterprise. The additional clues about people and places that exist in real life do not exist on the Web. Charming idiosyncrasies easily become annoying in the absence of a personal smile or handshake.

Look at everything in the organization and on the Web sites as if you were seeing it for the first time and with no knowledge of the people involved. And question everything.

Maintaining Enthusiasm

Web projects typically start out with tremendous enthusiasm: this is, after all, something very new. That enthusiasm is simply not going to be maintained over the life of a project. You need to recognize this and to budget your resources accordingly.

It is normal for there to be slumps in the course of any project; with the strain of Web time, those slumps may come more suddenly and be deeper. Be prepared.

Also, remember that the Web is more public than most other endeavors. Accidents do happen, but they may be held up to ridicule by strangers. Try not to be surprised. You can do this by being careful and by being prepared.

Getting Rid of the "Web Project"

Finally, remember that your goal should be to get rid of the Web project. The heart of a Web-based enterprise is an integrated environment combining the Internet with traditional bricks and mortar. Unless yours is a startup company, you will need to work aggressively to integrate the two sides of your business. The longer they remain separate, the harder it will be to bring them together.

Summary

You have looked at your Web-based enterprise and its Web pages; you know how to discuss them in functional terms (no more vague or squishy comments about "look and feel"). You have seen how to manage your Web-based enterprise staff and how to plan for training and maintenance. You are ready to begin.

The final chapter of this book helps you do just that: go back to the beginning and actually start the work of inventing the Web-based enterprise.

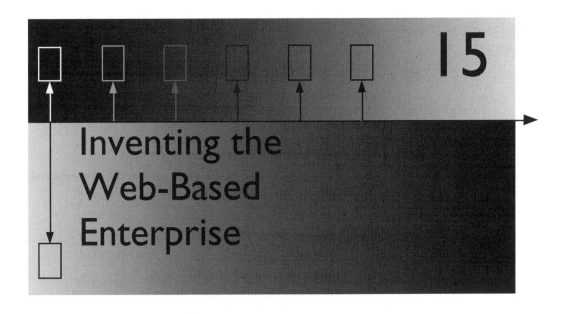

15

Inventing the Web-Based Enterprise

Your Web-based enterprise is a new venture. It has to be: the Web is only a decade old. Everyone who is working in your Web-based enterprise remembers very clearly a world without the Web. Old habits and ways of thinking die hard. There may well be people in your organization (or among your customers, suppliers, or others) who remember using carbon paper, typewriters, and telegrams.

As anyone who has learned a foreign language as an adult knows, there is a very strong tendency to think in the old context and then translate to the new. Linguistically, that produces such whoppers as "I feel happy as a violin" ("fit as a fiddle"). Technologically, that produces e-mail that is printed out and responded to in longhand (then transcribed to e-mail), online transactions confirmed with multiple telephone calls, and printed-out versions of Web sites (not individual pages).

This chapter provides a summary of the benchmarks and standards that have been described previously in the book. It brings together some of the themes that have been presented in Database-Driven Web Sites *and* Application Servers: Powering the Web-Based Enterprise. *First of all, it looks at how the Web-based enterprise fits into the changing world today.*

The Upheaval of Web-Based Enterprises

There is no way around it: the ideas behind the Web-based enterprise are radical and new to many people. The Internet itself makes barriers of time and space scarcely relevant—instantaneous access to people and information on the other side of the world is accepted today as the norm, and it is easily understood at least in concept.

The disintermediation that the Internet-based world creates is less well understood. People have—and expect to have—direct access across time and space to people and information that they need. Direct, unmediated access is something new to many people. In fact, it is fundamentally new to most of civilization.

Think for a moment of the efforts that have been made in the past to provide access to people and information across time and space. Writing itself is one of the earliest ways of conquering time and space—a written document (or tablet) can be carried from one place to another and stored for future reference. Consider how many legends and fairy tales involve searches Reflect, too, on how many of our governmental and societal structures exist in order to identify people in one way or another. (When a monarch imposes taxes or dispenses largesse, it is through a complex hierarchical structure that ends with the identification of individuals by people who know them—who, in turn, are known to the next higher level of officials, and so on in turn.)

The conquest of time and space, the ease of conducting searches, and the ability to identify people easily are all aspects of the Internet and the Web—and of the Web-based enterprise. If you look beyond the excitement of clicking on Web pages to the fundamental advances that they represent, you will see that—quite literally—you are dealing with radical changes the like of which have not been seen in most of civilization until now.

Perhaps the most important change that is occurring is in the disintermediation that affects political and power structures—corporate and governmental. The largest organizations on earth (major corporations and governments) can deal with individuals directly in a way that they could not before. This improves life for individuals and the large organizations; however, the vast numbers of people and organizations who have spent generations building disintermediation practices are—to say the least—disconcerted.

You ignore these changes at your risk. At some point—decades from now—they may be integrated into the way people live, work, and govern themselves. Until that time, however, a highly unstable environment will exist in which tremendous opportunities mix with enormous fears.

The true impact of technology on governments has only begun to be glimpsed; vast disintermediation may occur, making some forms of local and regional governments irrelevant. Already nongovernmental organizations are taking on increasingly large aspects of what were considered governmental operations.

Because this environment is so unstable, it is more important than ever to be focused on your objectives.

Objectives

Establish, question, and refine your objectives. The objectives you consider in a traditional enterprise are dwarfed by the opportunities of the Web.

Mission

What is it that you do? In both individual proprietorships and multinational corporations, review your mission. In looking at existing missions, critically evaluate how many of them involve intermediation. (Particularly in large and old organizations, intermediation has become a way of life; the Internet and the Web threaten that way of life directly.)

The rise of the Web-based enterprise—your own or someone else's—may make many of your organization's core functions irrelevant. Anticipate this and deal with it: circling the wagons and stomping your feet on the ground will not reverse the tide.

Some organizations find themselves almost totally defined by intermediation. Libraries, for example, rely on the relative scarcity of reading material and the difficulty of locating information for their very existence. (In the mid-nineteenth century, they worked with publishers in Britain to keep book prices high—and reading material scarce.) Today, the proliferation of reading material in low-cost electronic formats and the ease of locating information on line make the continuation of libraries in their present form quite doubtful. It may, however, herald a rather exciting rebirth of a new kind of library that involves more activities (such as reading groups and community classes). This type of situation presents itself in other intermediation-heavy operations such as regional governments, most forms of agentry, and warehouse distribution.

Scope

How much of your mission do you do or who do you do it for? By opening your enterprise to the Web—even on an internal network—you automatically open your operations to people who are distant in time and place. That, in turn, immediately raises questions about telecommuting—and that quickly lays the issue of hours of work on the table. All this from simply creating a few Web pages for employees to enter travel expenses, for example.

Expanding your scope is often a matter of simply letting people know that your enterprise is on line. (Sometimes it entails adding bandwidth or more servers.) It is very easy.

And this ease is precisely what you should be worried about: it is as easy for your competitors to do this as it is for you. (It may be easier for them, in fact.)

The existence of the Internet and the Web changes expectations for everybody. You cannot control what others do, but you can control what you do—and you can be ahead of the game in anticipating problems.

Truly, with the Web-based enterprise, there is no limit to the scope of your activities.

Place

Finally, the sense of place that you create for your Web-based enterprise is critical in refining people's expectations about your mission and its scope. The sense of place that you create is dependent almost totally on your online presence; the little cues that gargoyles on bricks-and-mortar buildings provide need to be provided by graphics and functionality on a Web page.

Remember that the graphics and functionality establish a sense of place whether you intend them to or not. Sloppiness and out-of-date material are the Internet equivalent of dusty shelves and rickety staircases.

Attributes of Web-Based Enterprises

Remember the world of Web-based enterprises that you have entered into. The bricks-and-mortar cues are gone; in their place are the following attributes.

Web Size

You cannot tell the size of a Web-based enterprise—your own or someone else's. This is the opportunity and the challenge for Web-based enterprises.

Web Time

Living in Web time (a 24/7 world where things are expected to happen instantaneously) is a change for most people. The rules have changed and they are not yet fully understood.

As noted in the previous chapter, as soon as you establish a Web presence, you need to start thinking about issues such as coverage—having certain people available at all hours of the day and night. This does not mean that some people work all the time: it means that you must determine who works when—and who doesn't. (In fact, determining who is not working at a given moment can be critical to avoiding burn-out.)

Web Space

The absence of "there" on the Web has impact on everything from taxation and customs laws to the languages of your Web pages. You control your enterprise's location in a transitory way that is irrelevant to bricks-and-mortar structures.

Flexibility

Finally, remember that Web-based enterprises are—and are expected to be—flexible.

Putting all of these attributes together means that you have turned a switch with regard to the way in which you and your people work.

Handling Your Data

In the 1970s and 1980s, it was all the corporate rage to create elaborate data dictionaries and data models for all an organization's data. By the time all of the laborious data modeling was finished, more often than not the business had changed—sometimes quite dramatically.

The Web, with its links, provides a way to manage large amounts of enterprise data in a way that has not been done before. Instead of constructing an enterprise-wide model, you can construct small, local models that interact via links. If you take this route, you can frequently achieve very significant results very quickly.

There are three steps to handling enterprise-wide data efficiently in this way.

Digitize

Digitize information as quickly as possible. If you can, avoid all paper: have the data entered directly via forms onto the Web and into a database.

Categorize

Avoid having to categorize or file data manually. Use forms and databases for data entry rather than e-mail; e-mail needs to be converted to mass storage in one way or another. (XML can be very helpful in categorizing data.)

One significant benefit of categorizing data with forms and a database is that the person providing the data—a client, a patient, a vendor, or a supervisor—frequently knows much more about the data than someone who traditionally would have categorized or entered the data.

Particularize Data

Get into the particulars of the data—its quality and authenticity, for example. The traditional way of establishing enterprise databases was to screen and massage data carefully so that only "good" data went into the database. This created vast intermediation efforts.

If you store data with information about its quality—verified, verified but doubtful, and so forth—you can avoid all of that. There are cases in which approximations are fine; in other cases, you need very good data. Store everything, well categorized, and with particulars about its quality, origin, and the like.

Many old-timers are reluctant to categorize or particularize data; they remember the days when disk storage was expensive and database management systems were slow. That has changed.

Handling Your Operations

If you follow the suggestions in the previous section, you will wind up with many data sources within your organization. Each source will have its own data, each will have its data categorized (perhaps with XML), and each will have particulars about the data quality and source.

Tolerate Ambiguity	The responsibility for using the data properly then moves into the operational area: your database operations are simply designed to store data and as much information about it as possible.
	Your databases will be inconsistent, and they will be—from an enterprise-wide perspective—unnormalized. However, they will be able to function quickly and easily. The operations and programs need to reflect these ambiguities, but they will be able to come on line much faster than if everything had to wait for everything to be perfect.
Use Links for Data Transfer	You can use links—either HTML links or programmatic links—to get to the data that you need. The Web model provides for the intermediation of software in providing data which itself is the result of a very simple request. The application server model (discussed in *Application Servers: Powering the Web-Based Enterprise*) lets you intervene as necessary to modify data.
	This is a looser form of linking than allowing remote applications to access databases. However, in its very looseness it works.

Making It Work

All of the tools and techniques discussed in these books help you to develop your Web-based enterprise: whether it is an old or a new enterprise, and whether it consists of thousands of workers or just yourself on one evening a week.

Here are some final tips to make it work.

Set Achievable Goals (and Make Them)

One of the lessons learned in the computer world is that large-scale projects that require many components to come on line together and work properly often fail or are abysmally late. The Web is ideally suitable to small-scale projects and large-scale projects that consist of links among smaller projects.

Use this architecture to create projects that you can be assured of finishing. People with experience in the development of Web sites can almost always predict whether a site will open on time or be late—or abandoned. At a first meeting, the complexity of the site's design and the willingness of the Web team to discuss rather than make decisions give it away.

Keep Your Eyes Open

People all over the world are building Web sites and creating Web-based enterprises. Watch what is going on—within your sphere of interest as well as elsewhere. The fundamental issues of creating a Web-based enterprise that is a bank are in many ways similar to those of creating a Web-based enterprise that is a manufacturer of hardware.

Listen to Users

Particularly when your sites are first made public, there will be problems. Listen to users—particularly those who have problems. It does not matter if the problem is yours or the user's: work to avoid it in the future.

It is amazing how many user complaints are ignored by Web designers who are insulted or offended. You may ultimately discard this input, but do not ignore it.

Use Your Own Site

Finally, make certain that you use your own site. It almost seems ludicrous that anyone would not do so, but experience has shown that this can be true. Do not just check it out periodically (to see if your picture is still on the home page). Attempt to purchase something; try using the feedback buttons. Make sure it works and that you can do what you think you should be able to do with it.

Summary

This chapter recapitulates the descriptions of the Web-based enterprise that you found at the start of this book. At this point you should have definite ideas as to your own Web-based enterprise's objectives (its mission, place, and scope) as well as its particular attributes (its Web size and time).

You have seen throughout this book how essential it is to identify and organize your Web-based enterprise's data. You have also seen how critical it is to manage your operations flexibly and with a tolerance of the ambiguity that comes with a Web-based enterprise.

The challenges of the Web-based enterprise are many; those who are successful are the people who understand the structure beneath the design and the logic behind the promotional hype.

This book should give you the confidence to follow your hunches and instincts where appropriate. It also should show you what you can and should do yourself and what you need to delegate or refer to others with particular skills. Most of all, it should get you thinking about what a Web-based enterprise is and how you can make yours the best one it can possibly be.

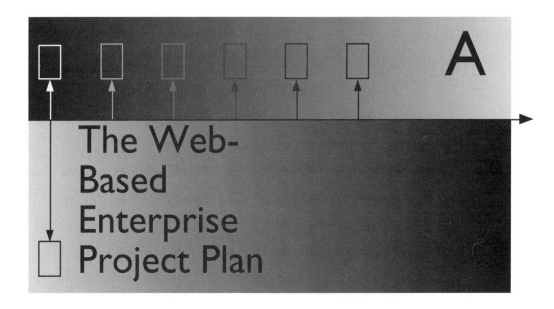

A

The Web-Based Enterprise Project Plan

As with any major project, the devil is in the details—and there are many, many details for Web-based enterprises. You can organize the issues and ideas presented in this book in any way that you want; all that matters is that you do so and make certain that everyone understands what needs to be done.

Note that these are suggestions. Modify them and customize them for your own organization.

Creating a Web Site Registry

You need to keep track of your enterprise's Web presence(s). You can rely on a directory listing of the files on your site, but that is scarcely sufficient for tracking changes, and it certainly doesn't help you deal with pages and files that have not yet been developed.

The information that you need to maintain can be stored in a database, a spreadsheet, a word-processing program, or even on paper. You can view this record-keeping as a burden; on the other hand, you can view it as an opportunity to implement your own database-driven Web site. It can be an experimentation engine and training ground for new staff. Take it as your task to implement a Web site registry that can be accessed by any team member using the browsers and networking facilities that your site will use. Find the problems and break the design on your own internal management site—not on your users' site!

First, you need an overall objective and plan; this can easily fill one word-processing document page (it should not be much bigger).

The data that you track will depend on your enterprise, but it typically will fall into three groups (each one can easily be an SQL table):

- Page information
- Change information
- Management information and contacts

If you are building your own internal Web site for management, the home page should contain the objective and plan with links to the three other tables.

Overall Objective and Plan

Set the site's mission, scope, and place as described in "Designing and Implementing the Site" starting on page 223. Do not just pay lip service to this: think it through. While you do not want to embark on a months-long process of introspection, you do need to make certain that your objective is correct and that your plan can be carried through.

You need to do whatever reality checks you can at this point. Many people get the objective right but neglect to consider whether their resources will support it. You do not need to establish elaborate budgets to get benchmark estimates of costs. Make certain that your plan—that is, your budget, resources, and timetable—matches your objective. If there is a discrepancy, adjust one—or both.

Page and Site Information

Chapters 6 and 7 describe the parts and characteristics of pages and sites. Go through the lists and determine which parts and characteristics matter to you; use that list as the basis of the fields in your page and site information table.

Note that when in doubt you should include parts and characteristics. You may leave them blank, but in the future you may need to support multiple languages, extended media types, and so forth.

Add to the parts and characteristics the function of each page and subsite.

Make certain that each record in the page and site table has a unique identifier: that means having a unique identifier for each page and subsite in your project. (As noted previously, those identifiers should be meaningless—simple serial numbers are usually best.)

Change Information	You will constantly be changing your site and subsite. Refer to Table 12-1, "Fields for a Problem Report," on page 243 for the data that you need.
Management Information and Contacts	The final table provides information on all the people on the project. This can be a standard database table—you may have the appropriate data already stored. Make certain that this information is not scattered among the other tables in your Web site registry.

Make certain that your contact information includes the 24/7 support that is needed on the Web. One way of doing this is to provide links within the contact table so that each person is linked to another person who covers the first person's responsibilities. Of course, if you do this, you need to make certain that your management structures are in place so that at least one person is available at all times. Coverage is essential in supporting Web sites. |

Step-by-Step Checklist for Managing a Web-Based Enterprise

The step-by-step checklist in Table A-1 is meant as an example from which you can create your own checklist. The basic steps described in this book are prioritized for common Web-based enterprise projects.

Many of the highest priority tasks are done relatively infrequently (you do not change your site's objective or hire staff every day). A number of them are ongoing—and just because they should be routine does not mean that they should not be given the highest priority. (Training is in this category.)

Keep an eye out for those tasks that you or your team members prefer to avoid. Maybe you particularly enjoy fiddling with hardware (or maybe you do not). In either case, make certain that your preferences do not distract from other tasks that need to be done.

Each task needs to be assigned to an individual and to have a completion date (one-time or recurring) assigned to it. As with the Web site registry, use this as an opportunity to implement an internal Web site with dynamically updated data.

Task	Scope	Priority
Assign Responsibility/Hire Staff	Overall	1
Create Job Descriptions	Overall	1
Do Performance Appraisals (Ongoing)	Overall	1
Set Objective	Site	1
Set Mission	Site	1
Set Place	Site	1
Set Scope	Site	1
Training	Overall	1
Domain Name Registration and Maintenance	Site	2
Set Privacy Policy	Site Policy	2
Set Security Policy	Site Policy	2
Set Site Design (Unified, Distributed, Fragmented)	Site/Subsite Design	2

TABLE A-1. Checklist for a Web-Based Enterprise

Task	Scope	Priority
Enforce Page Characteristics Values	Page Implementation	3
Enforce Page Part Values	Page Implementation	3
Maintenance Plan	Overall	3
Privacy Implementation	Page/Subsite Implementation	3
Security Implementation	Page/Subsite Implementation	3
Set Page Characteristics and Values	Site/Subsite Design	3
Set Page Function	Page/Subsite Implementation	3
Set Page Parts and Values	Site/Subsite Design	3
Site Layout (Mirrors, Location, etc.)	Site	3
Test Suite	Site/Subsite Design	3
Determine Gatekeeper Technology	Site/Subsite Design	4
Dynamic Web Page Support (Choose JSP, ASP, Application Server, etc.)	Site	4
Implement Gatekeeper Technology	Site/Subsite Implementation	4
Select Communications from Users (Forms, E-mail)	Site	4
Select Communications to Users (Inline, Linked, Downloadable/PDF)	Page	4
Site Hardware Support	Site	4

TABLE A-1. Checklist for a Web-Based Enterprise (Continued)

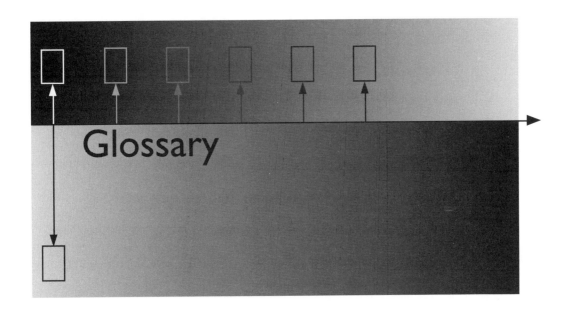

Glossary

24/7 Twenty-four hours a day, seven days a week. Pronounced "twenty-four seven" or "twenty-four by seven." Used in reference to operations that must always be available; 24/7 often connotes attended operation of a system.

Active Server Pages (ASP) Active Server Pages combine HTML and scripts (in JavaScript, VBScript, or Perlscript). The scripts run on the server and HTML is sent to the client. This Microsoft technology relies on their server products; however, third parties have ported the technology to other environments (such as Unix).

API
An application programming interface (API) is the specification of inputs and outputs that allows programmers to write code that interacts with existing software.

applet
A small piece of computer code that is typically downloaded from a Web site as part of a Web page. Applets are often written in machine-independent languages (such as Java). They may be used to enhance the user experience with animation; they may also be used for editing and data access. Scripts (written in Visual Basic, JavaScript, and Perl) are similar to applets, but they contain instructions that the browser must fully convert. Applets contain partially generated computer code, and require less work from the browser.

application
A term used to refer to a computer program (as in a "word processing application") or to a process developed for a specific functional purpose (as in "the insurance claim processing application").

application server
Software that typically interacts with a database and template files in order to produce dynamic HTML for database-driven applications. Also called "middleware."

browser
Programs such as Netscape Communicator, Microsoft Internet Explorer, or NCSA Mosaic that let you explore the World Wide Web. Proprietary systems such as America Online and private organizations' software may use their own browsers.

CGI (common gateway interface)
The standard for communication between a Web server application and other programs. CGI files are often stored in the cgi-bin directory on a server.

controls
Parts of Web-based forms that you can manipulate. They include buttons, text areas, and drop-down menus.

CRT screens
Cathode ray tubes. The devices used to view computer data before flat-panel displays were invented.

data element
An entry in a database structure, such as age, address, or price. Each data element has a name; a data element usually

has many values in a database—each value corresponds to one observation, record, or individual.

database
A collection of data that is organized for easy storage and retrieval. Databases are managed by database software such as Oracle or Microsoft Access.

database project
A user-created set of database data that includes data entry screens, documentation, assistance, and reports.

database software
Software that manages databases. Some products are Microsoft Access, DB2, Oracle, Sybase, and FileMaker Pro.

DBMS
Database management system. Database software.

DNS
Domain name system tables. The Internet addressing tables that translate domain names to IP addresses. DNS tables are maintained at central Internet sites ("base servers"); their contents are propagated throughout the Internet as routine addressing is carried out.

domain
A named location on the Internet that corresponds to a specific IP address. The connection between the domain name (such as www.philmontmill.com) and an IP address (such as 205.231.144.10) is maintained by DNS tables.

DHCP
Dynamic host configuration protocol. A local networking protocol that assigns variable IP addresses to computers as they attempt to connect to the Internet.

e-commerce
The use of the Internet for commercial purposes such as buying and selling goods and information. E-commerce Web sites are often powered by databases.

factoring
The process of separating interface programming from application programming. Factoring is a necessary step in producing programs that can be scripted.

fields
A single piece of data within a database record. (Also called a data element.) The contents of a field or data element are data

values. A field (such as "age") may have many values (reflecting the ages of individuals whose information is contained in the database).

firmware

Computer instructions that are stored in a hardware device (rather than in memory or on a medium such as disk or CD-ROM). Firmware is normally installed when the computer is assembled. It may be upgraded later, but is generally regarded as fixed and immutable for most purposes.

flat file

A traditional computer file (such as text or graphics) that does not have the indexing and fast retrieval features of database files.

FTP

File transfer protocol. The Internet protocol used to transfer files between computers.

Gopher

The Internet text-based menu system for organizing data. Largely replaced by the World Wide Web.

GIF

Graphical interchange format. A format (including image compression) that is used primarily for computer-generated images on the Internet. Compare to JPEG.

hot

Part of a computer image that responds to a mouse click. Buttons and links on Web pages are hot.

HTML

HyperText Markup Language. The language used to design and format Web pages. If you use a graphical Web page editor, you may rarely see raw HTML.

IDE

Integrated development environment. A graphically based environment that contains a program text editor, compiler, linker, and debugger. IDEs allow programmers to switch between writing and testing code; often, changes can be made to source code while the application is running.

intranet

A network that uses Internet protocols but which is not open to the general public.

IP address — A set of four numbers that identify an Internet node. The numbers are separated by dots as in 205.231.144.10. IP addresses are often associated with domain names which are easier for people to deal with.

ISP — Internet Service Providers typically provide access to the Internet: they are the companies at the other end of the phone line or cable connection. Internet service providers typically offer services in addition to connectivity such as database hosting, Web-site hosting, e-mail, and so forth. ISPs bundle such services, but many organizations use a variety of vendors to handle the different services.

JPEG — A format (including image compression) that is typically used for natural images (photographs, for example), on the Internet. JPEG compression is "lossy"—each repeated saving of a JPEG file loses part of the image data.

key — A field that is used to retrieve or identify data. Keys are usually indexed in a database by the database software for fast retrieval.

legacy — Old systems, files, and databases that need to be incorporated into current processes.

LAN — Local area network. A network within a limited area (room, floor, building, airplane, or space station). LANs may be connected to other networks, but themselves are self-contained and are not subject to public regulation.

meta-data — Data about data. Meta-data includes names of fields (as distinct from their values).

middleware — Software that exists between database data and user interface manipulation. Often used as a synonym for "application servers."

MIME — Multipurpose Internet Mail Extension. A format that allows for non-text data to be incorporated into messages.

normalization

A set of rules for structuring database data to avoid duplication, improve efficiency, and minimize operational problems.

object-oriented programming

A programming architecture in which small units—objects—are employed. Each object is self-contained, and its interfaces are well-defined. Objects are created (instantiated) as needed and communicate with one another through messages or function calls. In object-oriented programming, global variables and program-wide operations are avoided.

ODBC

Open Database Connectivity is a language that lets data sources (databases, flat files, spreadsheets, etc.) communicate with applications. It is based on SQL queries. ODBC is installed on a computer as an extension to the operating system; ODBC drivers for specific types of data sources are available from various vendors. The use of ODBC makes it possible for applications to communicate at a high level with data sources about which they have little knowledge.

plug-in

A section of code that can be added to an application (such as a Web server). It adheres to the application's standards and is called by the application as necessary. Plug-ins may be used to handle database access. They are often developed by third parties (that is, not by the Web server developer). In addition to Web servers, plug-ins are often used to add functionality to graphics programs such as Photoshop and QuarkXPress.

port

The entity on a network node that communicates with other network entities. A given computer typically has a variety of numbered ports. Each port number is assigned to a specific service (for example, http is typically port 80). The communications link for the computer can support a variety of ports. All messages for a given port are routed to a specific application (such as a Web server for port 80).

program

Also known as an application or application program. The software that performs tasks using hardware and communications devices.

protocols The rules governing communication between and among hardware and software components.

query A request to a database for information. Queries may also be used to add information to a database. Today, most queries are formulated using SQL.

record A given data instance—one student, one shopping order, etc. Each data instance consists of the data values for each of the fields in the table.

RFC Request for Comments. Internet standards are developed collaboratively within the Internet community. Requests for Comments are issued and input accepted until a standard is set. These standards may later be modified or replaced. RFCs are numbered. For the ultimate word on specific Internet concepts, consult the RFCs. You can find them in many places including www.internic.net; you can also search for "RFC" with a search engine.

scalability The ability of a system (hardware or software) to be enlarged or decreased in size. Scalability often refers to large changes in size such as going from a Web site that supports 50 transactions a day to one that supports 50,000 transactions a day. Typically, such drastic changes have stressed hardware and software. Desktop software often does not scale up; likewise, enterprise software does not scale down.

schema The structure of a database table.

search engine A Web site or application that lets you search the Internet using words or combinations of words. Search engines are contrasted with prepared indices in which you must know the identification code for the item you wish to retrieve.

session For dial-in computer users, the connection that is established over a telephone line and a modem with an Internet service provider. For other users, the connection that is established between log in of a password and user ID and log out.

SGML Structured Generalized Markup Language. Languages that combine formatting and content in a text-based document. HTML is an example of an SGML.

site A registered location on the Internet; a site normally has a domain name. Sites may contain subsites that may or may not be located on the same computer.

SQL Structured Query Language. A common language used to describe and manipulate relational databases.

Standards Information Excellent glossaries of terms are available on the Internet. One of the best for telecommunications issues is *Federal Standard 1037C: Glossary of Telecommunications Terms*. It is available at http://ntia.its.bldrdoc.gov/fs-1037/dir-001/_0067.htm.

W3C—The World Wide Web Consortium develops standards for Web protocols including HTML. You can access W3C at http://www.w3.org/.

SQL standards can be obtained from the American National Standards Institute at http://web.ansi.org.

Information about standards and terminology can also be obtained from vendors of specific products.

stateless Usually used in reference to HTML, stateless refers to the fact that the server does not store information about the client between transmissions. As a result, each message sent to the server must contain all of the data that the server will need to process the transaction.

system A non-specific term that can apply to a specific operation ("payroll system"), hardware (computer system), or application software. A source of confusion in many cases.

table In HTML, tables are used to organize information into rows and columns. Forms are often used to collect data from users; tables are often used to display results of database queries. In relational databases, tables refer to the organized structure of data. Rows (records) and columns (fields) contain observations for each individual/instance and data element.

teletype 1950s and 1960s data entry and display devices. Teletypes use continuous rolls of paper. They contain mechanisms to advance the paper (but not to reverse it). A number of controls are still part of standard communications protocols (top of page, top of form, etc.).

template file A file containing part of a Web page. Written in HTML, template files have special elements that enable an application server to merge dynamic information with the prepared HTML in the template.

text document A document containing only visible text characters (no graphics, no applets, etc.).

transaction A process that may consist of a number of database accesses (retrievals, entries, and updates), but which is considered as a single unit. Transactions can typically be cancelled or rolled back: in those cases, all parts of the transaction are cancelled or rolled back.

URL Uniform resource locators. An Internet address.

value The contents of a field in a given record; alternatively, the contents of a row in a given column.

Web server A program that provides Web pages on demand to clients. A Web server is assigned a port on a computer; all messages that come to that computer's port go to the Web server. A Web server may also be the computer that runs a Web server. By using several port numbers, a single Web server computer can run a number of Web server programs.

Webmaster The person responsible for a Web site.

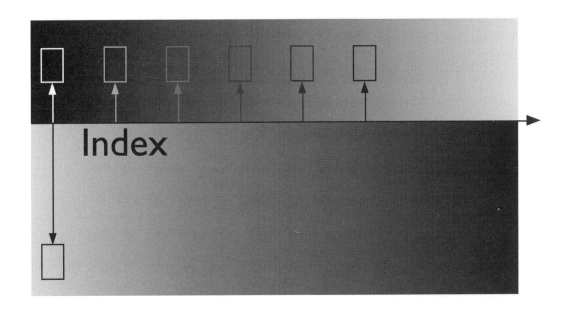

Index

A

access (security) 52
access controls
    explicit 54
    implicit 53
Acrobat Distiller 181
Acrobat Reader 181
action buttons 126, 147, 149, 150, 162
ads 124, 147, 149, 150, 161
advertisements 124, 147, 149, 150, 161
ambiguity 295
Anarchie 95
Archie 95

ASP 90
authentication 47
    end of 51
author 129, 148, 149, 151, 162

B

bandwidth 132, 167
basic product information 217
Bezos, Jeffrey 4
BODY element **93**
books 280

Principal entries and definitions are shown in **bold**.

X

About the Author

JESSE FEILER is Software Director of Philmont Software Mill. He has served as consultant, author, and/or speaker for organizations including the Federal Reserve Bank of New York, Prodigy, Kodak, Young & Rubicam, The Josef and Anni Albers Foundation, and Yale University Press.

His technical credits span mainframes to personal computers including machines from IBM, Apple, Burroughs, and Control Data; databases from IBM, Burroughs, Oracle, Microsoft, and Claris; object-oriented frameworks including MacApp and OpenStep; languages ranging from Fortran, Algol, and Cobol to Pascal, C++, Java, and Objective-C; as well as a host of end user and productivity tools from vendors including Microsoft, Apple, IBM, and Claris.

He is the author of a number of books including *Database-Driven Web Sites* (Morgan Kaufmann, 1999); *Application Servers: Powering the Web-Based Enterprise* (Morgan Kaufmann, 2000); *Mac OS X Developer's Guide* (Morgan Kaufmann, 2000); *Mac OS X: The Complete Reference* (Osborne/McGraw-Hill, 2001); *Perl 5 Programmer's Notebook* (Prentice-Hall, 1999); *FileMaker Pro 4 and the World Wide Web* (FileMaker Press, 1999); *Automating FileMaker Pro* (Morgan Kaufmann, 2000); *Cyberdog* (AP Professional, 1996); *ClarisWorks 5.0: The Internet, New Media, and Paperless Documents* (Claris Press, 1998); *Essential OpenDoc* (with Anthony Meadow, Addison-Wesley, 1996); and *Real World Apple Guide* (M&T Books, 1995).

Together with Barbara Butler, he wrote *Finding and Fixing Your Year 2000 Problem: A Guide for Small Businesses and Organizations* (AP Professional, 1998; Sybex Verlag, 1999 [German edition], RocketEdition [eBook], 1999). They also wrote *Y2K Bible, Procrastinator's Edition* (IDG Books, 1999). They have spoken, written, and consulted extensively on the Year 2000 problem.

Jesse Feiler serves on the boards of the HB Playwrights Foundation, the Philmont Public Library, and the Mid-Hudson Library System. He is the 1997 recipient of the Velma K. Moore Award given by the New York State Association of Library Boards for "exemplary service and dedication to libraries."

Philmont Software Mill is located on the Web at www.philmontmill.com.